ORCHIDS
SIMPLIFIED

ORCHIDS SIMPLIFIED

An indoor gardening guide

BY HENRY JAWORSKI

PRINCIPAL PHOTOGRAPHERS

ALAIN MASSON

CHARLES MARDEN FITCH

KJELL SANDVED

CHAPTERS PUBLISHING LTD. SHELBURNE, VT 05482

To Linda,
a sometimes orchid widow.

Published by
Chapters Publishing Ltd.
2031 Shelburne Road
Shelburne, Vermont 05482

Library of Congress
Cataloguing-in-Publication Data

Jaworski, Henry, 1945-
Orchids simplified : an indoor gardening guide /
by Henry Jaworski.
p. cm.
Includes index.
ISBN 0-9631591-5-1 : $24.95 —
ISBN 0-9631591-4-3 (softcover) : $19.95
1. Orchid culture. 2. Orchids.
3. Indoor gardening. I. Title.
SB409.J38 1992
635.9 ' 3415—dc20
92-15078 CIP

Trade distribution by
Firefly Books Ltd.
250 Sparks Avenue
Willowdale, Ontario
Canada M2H 2S4

Printed and bound in Canada by
Friesen Printers
Altona, Manitoba

Design Director: Hans Teensma/Impress, Inc.
Art Director: Marcy Kass
Assistant Editor: Deidre Stapleton
Production Editor: Susan Dickinson

Cover photograph:
Cymbidiums by Scott Camazine

ACKNOWLEDGMENTS

I'D LIKE to acknowledge years of advice from various members of the Southern Ontario Orchid Society and especially Doug Kennedy for his help with this book. To Bob Botkin, who has always been a great sounding board, and James Bateman, whose book of the beautiful orchids of Mexico and Guatemala was an inspiration.

Opening page: ***Sophronitis coccinea 'Edelweiss.'***

Previous pages: ***Dendrobium cuthbertsonii.***

Right: ***Calypso orchids growing wild in the Pacific Northwest.***

Following pages: ***Paphiopedilum bellatulum.***

Contents

Why Orchids?
While other plants provide a pleasant background to my life, orchids have burrowed into its center . . . 11

Blooming Legacy
An orchid by any other name . . . 17

Orchid Primer
If you can grow a philodendron, you can grow a phalaenopsis . . . 25

Your First Plants
Caveat emptor: What to buy and where to find it . . . 33

A Place to Grow
Let there be light, but not too much . . . 43

Potting
Containing your enthusiasm . . . 51

The Great Outdoors
A summer in the backyard can result in an autumn bounty of blooms . . . 59

Orchids You Can Grow
A sampler of popular species . . . 69

The Greenhouse Effect
Finding a permanent home for your hobby . . . 103

Increasing the Bounty
An introduction to propagation techniques . . . 109

Life Without a Home
As habitats vanish, orchids face an uncertain future in the wild . . . 117

Appendices
Glossary . . . 126
Sources . . . 130
Further Reading . . . 134
Photography Credits . . . 137
Index . . . 139

CHAPTER ONE

Why Orchids?

While other plants provide a pleasant background to my life, orchids have burrowed into its center.

I BEGAN growing orchids for the obscurest of reasons. It was the impending birth of my first daughter, Zoë, in the mid-1970s. Everywhere around me were the signs of nest building: cribs, paint in the baby's room, stockpiles of strange foods and, of course, the relentless feeling of new growth and beginnings. I wanted to be part of it. I wanted to grow something new and exciting too. I'd grown outdoors for years, so the solution had to be in gardening. At the time, we lived in the center of Toronto, near one of those late-Victorian botanical gardens that have since gone out of fashion. On regular walks there, I would admire the wonderful variety of tropical plants, especially the orchids. I knew they were orchids because they grew on the branches of trees or twined cunningly along moss-covered walls.

Even out of flower, the exotic bulbs with fat leaves looked as if they had been waxed and polished by nature. Their thick, white roots, with the most delicately green tips imaginable, crawled over the outside of the pots and wooden baskets in which the plants grew. They were infinitely more exciting than any mere soil-growing plant.

This is a strange phenomenon I've observed in other new orchid growers. It is not just the flowers they find irresistible. Every part of the plant seems to elicit the most uncommon fascination. The newly bitten orchidophile wants to touch orchids, gaze at them and just admire their unusualness. Ultimately, he or she also wants to unpot them, divide them and make more plants.

***Angraecum sesquipedale*, above; *Burma's Cymbidium tracyanum*, opposite.**

Seeing those plants suspended over lush green pathways at Allan Gardens made me want to find out more about orchids. Getting to know orchids these days is much easier. Orchid plants

Native to Australia, Dendrobium phalaenopsis is now popular among home growers.

are often sold at garden centers, and more people are growing orchids. Back then, a few hard-to-find volumes outlining growing procedures for greenhouses were the only books available at local libraries. I had no greenhouse and wanted to grow orchids right away—on my windowsill, if I could.

Soon, I was getting catalogs from orchid companies that advertised in the backs of conventional gardening magazines. You might be familiar with the sort of thing: three orchids and easy instructions for $19.95. The three orchids—tiny seedlings barely out of their nursery flasks—were more suited to life-support systems than my windowsill. In this manner, with one or two exceptions, I became an orchid killer before I became an orchid grower.

Bountiful displays of flowers–and sage advice–can be found at local orchid shows.

The discovery that others shared my newfound enthusiasm went a long way toward saving the world's orchids from my pitiful experiments. I learned that there was a local orchid society which met once a month. Not being a joiner in the conventional sense, I imagined the worst: androgynous maiden ladies in winter-weight tweeds and slightly gaga gentlemen repeating some dictum over and over. As it turned out, I was the only one in tweeds going gaga over the fabulous variety of plants on display. The society members were very generous with their advice, and offers to show me their collections steadied my nerve long enough for me to realize that I could do it too.

The need for the reassurance of experienced growers is a common trait most newcomers to the hobby possess. Orchids have such a baggage of mythology that even the most confident grower likes to check with a successful colleague—or brag a little about his or her own growing ability.

That mythology surrounding orchids—the fabled black orchid; the unique universal desirability of orchids—at once attracts us and keeps beginners from realizing soon enough how easy orchids really are.

The first orchid to reach Europe was brought by the Spaniards in 1510 from their Latin American colonies. It was vanilla, the most popular confection flavor in the world. Yes, vanilla is an orchid. Actually, it's the cured seedpod of an orchid. The Spaniards found the local Indians mixing it in drinks with another South American introduction—chocolate.

The orchids we cultivate today didn't begin to appear in collections until after Captain James Cook's voyages to the tropical areas of the world. Cook's botanist, Joseph Banks, found breadfruit to feed slaves in the colonies, but he also brought back orchids. By 1789, there were 15 exotic orchid species listed in the records at the Royal Botanic Gardens (Kew Gardens), in London, and the rest of Europe was not far behind.

But the pesky things kept dying, many on the long voyages from the colonies or in the stifling hothouses mistakenly designed for their encouragement. Greenhouses for the care of orchids were called "stoves," because of the relentless and suffocating humidity they offered their occupants. Victorian garden workers avoided entering them if they could.

The voyages of Captain James Cook, **right,** *led to the discovery of orchids that are still cultivated today.* **Below,** ***Dendrobium densiflorum.***

Few orchids survived, and those that did became even more desirable in light of their rarity.

Here's how a Mr. R. Glendinning presented his growing method—standing the potted plants on wet stone benches that dripped water on hot pipes—in the *Gardener's Magazine* in 1835: "[this] produces a constant evaporation of steam. As the plants are surrounded by water, this prevents the migration of wood lice

and also tends to increase the humidity of the atmosphere of the house. A vessel of water is kept on the cover of the boiler, with a syringe; and two or three times in the course of the day, according to the weather, the plants are slightly moistened with this warm water. By this mode of treatment and by admitting very little air at this end of the house, I have been enabled to flower a number of species." Not more than once, I would think, from his description.

Not until 1845, when Belgian collector Jean Linden—who had travelled in South and Central America—brought back reports of the actual conditions where orchids grew, did Europe begin to understand how to cultivate orchids. Air was introduced to the plants. Darkened greenhouses were scraped of their coatings, the heat was turned down, and the orchids thrived.

The 1800s provided gardeners with a cornucopia of new plants from Europe's tropical colonies. Keen competition developed among amateur growers to possess the finest and rarest plants. It wasn't enough that orchids would arrive by ship in London or Liverpool and be sold at auction in huge quantities. Eminent and wealthy collectors financed private expeditions, and it is reported that it cost up to £3,000 a year to maintain one collector in the field in 1870; as much as three well-off middle-class Victorian families earned.

Rex Stout's fictional detective Nero Wolfe, to my mind, personifies the ideal orchid grower. The premise in the popular mysteries was that Wolfe solved complicated crimes without ever leaving his midtown New York brownstone. The reason he did this, as Archie Goodwin, his faithful legman, frequently observed when chronicling the details of the latest case in his diary, was that he was supporting his orchid collection. Yes, that was Wolfe's sole reason for being, as any close reading of the text will attest. Oh, sure, there was talk of beer and good food prepared by Fritz, his personal cook, but it was to Theodore, Wolfe's gardener, who never took part in solving the mysteries, that Wolfe retreated twice every day, never to be disturbed on pain of some terrible fate, as Archie often noted. I can't believe it was Theodore who was the attraction. Wolfe's inspiration must have been the orchids.

***Masdevallia militaris*, above, *originated in the Columbian highlands. The aptly named golden chain orchid*, opposite.**

My own love affair with orchids has not abated in the 17 years since I paid five dollars for my first plant. I still thrill to the sight of a new orchid I've never seen before. And, fortunately, there are many of those. While other plants provide a pleasant background to my life, orchids have burrowed into its center. I've never met an orchid I didn't like, for one reason or another. They are a little like my teenage daughter, who started it all.

CHAPTER TWO

Blooming Legacy

An orchid by any other name . . .

IT MAY BE no accident that orchids have been so long associated with romance. The first orchids identified and named were members of the family that grows around the Mediterranean, the European genus *Orchis*. The distinctive shape of their characteristic twin underground tubers prompted their discoverers to name the plants after male sexual glands, which they resemble.

In the old days, medicine was an even more inexact science than it is today. One of the governing precepts was: if it looked like a body part, that's what it cured. In this way, orchids became identified with sexual healing and began to acquire an exotic reputation.

Those temperate Mediterranean orchids are not the ones growers cultivate on their windowsills today, although the sometimes less showy plants have their uses. In Turkey, a minor industry flourishes in which these underground tubers are dug and ground into a powder called salep. It is used to make a mucilaginous "ice cream," an ice cream so stiff that it must be eaten with a knife and fork—even on a summer day.

Many orchids grown today look as though they are quite unrelated to their humble temperate cousins. They come from countries roughly bounded by the tropics of Cancer and Capricorn, with the most numerous varieties occurring around the Equator. Those latitudes are said to be the cradle of all life, not just orchids. Here, plants have evolved for very specific purposes, often with very specific pollinators. That is one of the characteristics of orchids: each species has its own bee, moth, ant or bird to pollinate it. Some flowers are structured to accept only one pollinator and no other. Several authorities believe that these

***Epidendrum ciliare*, above; *Phalaenopsis violacea* from *Borneo*, opposite.**

Birds and bees: A hummingbird pollinates a sobralia,* top; *a bee visits a catasetum,* left. *To lure pollinators, a pleurothallis,* above, *resembles an insect.

orchids mimic the tantalizing odors which attract insects intent on sexual congress.

Physically, all orchids, no matter how different they look, have three traits in common: three sepals (the outer sheath of the bud), three petals and a column, a fleshy extension that combines the reproductive organs of stamens and pistils in one rather handy device. No other family of flowers has such a structure.

Here's how it works: At the front of the column sits the pollen, usually a couple of waxy, yellow balls held together by a membrane that ends with a sticky patch. When the insect alights on the flower, its intention is to move to the rear of the blossom, where an enticing odor urges "come hither." The bee or moth is forced to brush against the column in its journey to the back of the flower. The sticky "foot" is nature's version of space-age glue. Just one touch and it adheres, usually to the insect's back, abdomen or legs, and the pollen grains come with it. According to one theory, some flowers contrive to hit specific parts of the body of the pollinator, depending on the destination of the pollen.

Behind the pollen is a sticky indentation meant to receive pollen from an orchid of the same type. Between these two stations, nature provides another membrane that keeps the insect from fertilizing the orchid with its own pollen.

Like everything else, there are exceptions to this rule. Some orchids are cleistogamous, or self-pollinating. I remember seeing such orchids in Costa Rica, where they grew in not very tall trees near the Pacific Ocean. The flowers didn't open at all. Their buds simply parted a little in the middle, and the orchids self-pollinated without the aid of insects.

The other two characteristics of orchids—three sepals and three petals—are difficult to distinguish in some species. Paphiopedilums, for instance, have a modified lip that combines two petals into a pouch resembling an old-fashioned lady's slipper. So does its North American cousin, the pink lady's-slipper (*Cypripedium reginae*). *Coryanthes*, the so-called helmet orchid, has gone even further to create a bizarre puzzle of petals that forces a bee to slide down a ramp and get dunked in an apparently stupefying nectar. Only then is it allowed to crawl out "drunkenly." The bee does so, reeling from side to side and bumping into everything, which is when pollination takes place.

The Great Orchid Hobbyist on High has also seen fit to make orchids so environment-specific that their seeds, which are microscopic and almost totally devoid of nutrients, need a special fungus to predigest their food for them. Luckily, orchids are profligate in matters of gestation. They often produce millions of seeds,

This brassolaeliocattleya displays an orchid's telltale parts: three sepals and three petals, one modified into a lip.

so tiny they waft on the tropic wind, spreading themselves everywhere.

The phenomenon was noticed by Don Hipólito Ruiz, who was sent by the king of Spain to study the flora of Peru in 1777. While travelling between Xauxa and Tarma, in the Andean highlands, he observed: "The most plentiful of all the plants there belong to the orchid family. Their bulbs, growing on the surface, clothe and cover the driest and craggiest parts of the ground like cobblestones; and the varied colors of their strange and beautiful flowers tint that curious natural pavement." He was describing what is now known as *Maxillaria bicolor* but was called *caccacacca* by the native people, which meant "joined pavement."

Another odd thing about orchids is that when those tiny seeds do germinate, quite unlike the seeds of other plants, they puff up into a sort of green ball called a protocorm that eventually breaks roots and becomes a true plant.

The mobility of orchid seeds is said to be responsible for the large number of orchid species that exist. Those microscopic seeds are carried great distances from their place of origin. The resulting plants form remote colonies, called species swarms, which evolve to suit their new locations. That's one theory, anyway, to explain the huge variety of species among orchids, many of which are still being discovered and classified today.

Most of the orchids that hobbyists cultivate are epiphytic in one way or another. That is, they grow on tree branches or are attached to rocks, in which case they are called lithophytes. This characteristic of growing on things is an excellent adaptation in their environments, where the moisture content of the air differs little from the water content of the ground. The roots on the surface allow the plant

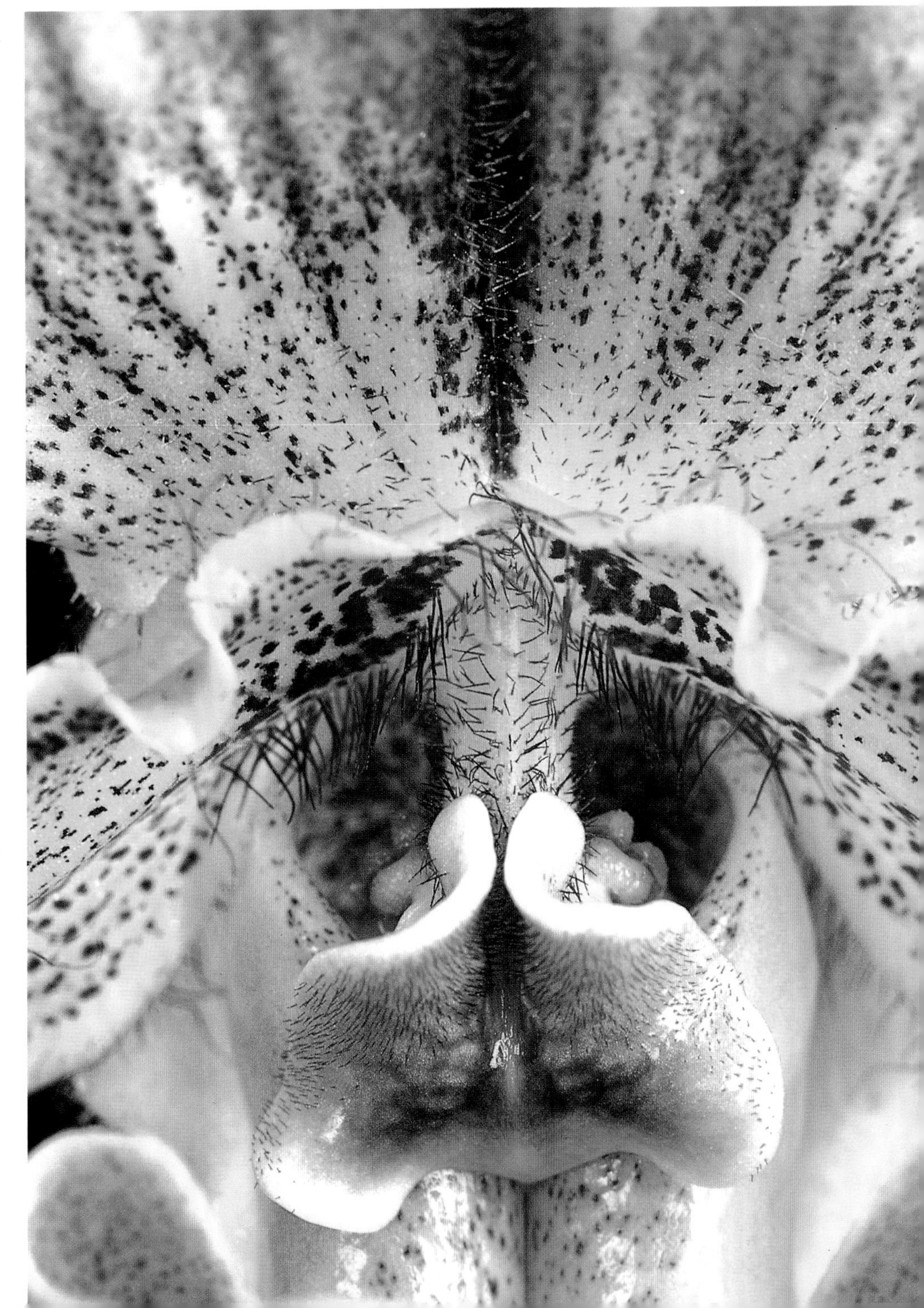

The reproductive organs of this paphiopedilum clearly show yellow pollen masses at the rear.

A jewel of the North American woodlands, the showy lady's-slipper is related to Asia's paphiopedilum orchids.

to absorb moisture and nutrients directly for maximum efficiency.

In parts of the world where monsoon conditions give way to months of arid dryness tempered only by a nighttime dew, some orchids have evolved pseudobulbs, or thickened stems, to store moisture. Other orchids have adapted further, with tougher epidermal growth that has allowed them to move into even drier conditions. It's no surprise that orchids are the largest family of flowering plants in the world.

Orchids generally grow in two ways: as a monopodial or a sympodial. If the orchid is a monopodial, a single stem grows continually in one direction, year after year, like Jack's beanstalk, adding a couple of leaves each season. A monopodial, which has no storage stem, is usually found in areas with a constant climate, where the plant has little need for storing food.

A sympodial orchid spreads by rhizomes, very much like the common bearded iris. But rather than lying on the ground and sending up a yearly fan of leaves, the orchid rests on a tree trunk, for instance, anchored to the bark by its roots. As the wet season approaches, new growths, or leads, grow vertically from the stems, forming leaf-covered branches. Depending on how dry the environment is, the branches will look more or less like pseudobulbs.

For me, one of the most fascinating aspects of orchids has been watching pseudobulbs form and grow. On cattleyas, for instance, a previously unobtrusive bulge at the base of the newest pseudobulb begins to swell. Soon, it splits, and a definite toelike bit of green pops out at ground level. Depending on the species, this rhizome moves along the surface of the soil or begins to grow vertically. Usually within a month or two, it has stretched up to duplicate itself. You'll soon know whether you are growing your plant well. It should be at least as large as the last pseudobulb. Maturity is followed by a rest period, during which

In many orchid species, new growth springs from pseudobulbs.

the plant decides whether it will flower for you. If you haven't reduced the size of the pseudobulb too much, it will bloom. Good growing is its own reward. If you can increase the size of the pseudobulb, you will often get plants with larger flowers and more of them.

Orchids are delightful to grow because they have no specific season. There is no winter, spring, summer or fall; no time when you stare moodily out the window and wonder when spring is going to come so that you can start digging in the ground. Orchids are governed by tropical imperatives: wet and dry seasons. During wet periods, they grow rapidly and mature. By the time it stops raining, they have reached maximum size for the conditions in which they are growing and go into a state of dormancy. The dry season is when flowering occurs. That's more or less what you should try to duplicate when growing orchids at home.

There is no mystery about what conditions orchids need to multiply happily. Like all plants, they require light, heat, fresh air, humidity, food and water, not necessarily in that order.

Most important is light. Orchids are light lovers. That's why so many of them are epiphytes. Growing in trees lifts them above the mass of plants that live on the forest floor. They seek those perfect conditions in the canopy of the rainforest. Even though there is no soil, the sheer square footage of vegetation at that height provides all the other factors needed for growth. They are surrounded by light. I've had orchids bloom for me that never bloomed before simply by moving them to sunnier parts of the greenhouse. It is a measure of orchids' adaptability that at home, we grow them in much less light than they can take in nature. If given half a chance, they will insist on growing. It's a well-known phenomenon that orchids on their last legs, abused by their owners, often leafless and almost rootless, will sometimes bloom one more time before they die.

In home growing, you should strive for maximum light given your other conditions. Like everything else in nature, orchid cultivation means living by the maxim of the golden mean: everything in balance.

You can tell from the leaf color how much light your orchids are getting. They will be a grass-green veering toward yellow if they are at the extreme bright end of their light potential. However, it is important how the

Growth Anatomy

Sympodial vs. Monopodial

Orchids generally grow in two ways: sympodial and monopodial. If the orchid is sympodial, such as the cattleya, **above left,** *it grows from a series of rhizomes. As the wet season approaches, new leads shoot vertically from the stems, forming leaf-covered branches. A monopodial orchid, such as the vanda,* **above right,** *produces a single stem that grows continually in one direction, year after year, adding a couple of leaves each season.*

The flowers of Oncidium altissimum are said to resemble a cloud of bees.

light is introduced. When you move your orchid from low- to high-light situations, it should be done gradually, just as you would move houseplants outdoors for the summer. Put them in shade for the first while, then slowly introduce them to sunlight.

But they will also bloom well with much less light. Orchids have been recorded growing in as little as 200 footcandles of light. It's worthwhile for any orchid grower who wants to see what that is like to take a walk in a patch of jungle, perhaps during a winter holiday in Mexico or somewhere in the Caribbean. Or do it nearer to home by standing in a forest in summer with many closely spaced deciduous trees. Yet plenty of usually small, obscure orchid species live in this kind of environment.

One of the most arresting sights I have ever seen was in such a woods in southern Mexico a few years ago. Rounding a bend on a gloomy forest path, I nearly jumped out of my skin when I thought I had walked headfirst into a swarm of killer bees hovering over the path. They looked big and brilliantly yellow and brown in the dim light. Only after I leapt back and stared at them for a moment did I realize that I hadn't encountered bees at all—it was a spray of oncidium flowers blooming from an overhanging branch.

It has been determined over the years that nearly all orchids require temperatures between 55 and 90 degrees F during the day and 50 to 70 degrees at night. The trick to growing them is to determine where your orchid fits on this scale. Growers have put orchids in three convenient categories: cool orchids from the higher mountains like a minimum of 50 degrees; medium orchids from the plateaus want 55 degrees; and warm orchids from the lowlands like 65 degrees. If you can keep your plants near these temperatures, you will be a happy grower.

A 19th-century botanical engraving clearly reveals this epidendrum's pseudobulb.

It is best at the beginning to choose orchids that match, more or less, the conditions in which you live. Don't try to grow cool orchids in Florida or southern California. Yes, I know some compulsively dedicated growers have done it, but at what price? Even with air conditioners or evaporative coolers in a greenhouse, the plants often succumb. The wrong ambient temperature seems to weaken them. Cool orchids can grow to perfection in the northeast or northwest parts of the country. So-called medium-temperature orchids often, with a little adaptation, grow just about everywhere. Most of us strive for this range so that we can grow as many varieties of orchids as possible.

Humidity is one of those topics, like watering, that cause endless discussion among orchid growers. How much should your plants get? It depends on the kind of orchid you have. As a rule, terrestrials need less than epiphytes. Orchids with thin leaves need more than plants with thick, fleshy leaves. Monopodials from warm climates prefer high humidity, while sympodials from these climates often require less. Cool growers seem to like a constant high humidity, day and night.

Sometimes, no matter what you do, an orchid fails to thrive. I have a plant of *Odontoglossum pendulum*, which in nature grows in the higher altitudes in Mexico. With head hung low, I admit that I have never flowered it in the decade I've owned it. But I have seen it flowered by someone else with more perfect conditions. I cherish that memory of branched spikes of large, soft pink blooms cascading downward from the basket. Someday, I think, that will be the way my plant will look, so each year I vary my culture just a little bit to try to induce those early-summer blooms.

CHAPTER THREE

Orchid Primer

If you can grow a philodendron,
you can grow a phalaenopsis.
Here's how.

HAVE YOU ever had a houseplant live, perhaps even flourish, on a windowsill? If so, it's safe to say your horticultural instincts are sharply enough honed to begin successful orchid cultivation—now.

I was a windowsill grower before I was an orchid grower. Like most of the avid orchid growers I have met, I was forced to resort to the rarefied atmosphere of my kitchen windowsill when the changing weather outside chased me from the garden. The windowsill is where I experimented with my potted-up summertime trophies, trying to duplicate the garden-club-exhibit quality of the luscious picture books. Often, I failed. Windowsills are wonderful experimental places. They are also very Darwinian: if you can't live with your neighbors, you'd better move elsewhere or die out. Even in this less-than-perfect atmosphere, some orchids thrive and prosper. Proof that orchids are made of stronger stuff.

There is one simple key to growing an orchid and having it bloom year after year. You have to choose the right kind. That is the biggest dilemma in orchid growing. The choice is so great. There are 20,000 to 50,000 species, depending on whether the taxonomists making the estimate are "lumpers" or "splitters." Orchids make up the largest family of flowering plants. That's not even counting the hundreds of thousands of crosses.

Above and opposite: ***Phalaenopsis species are renowned for being easy to cultivate.***

Naturally, some are more difficult to cultivate than others. But among experienced growers, there is one genus that is renowned for being particularly easy to grow on a windowsill in almost anyone's home: *Phalaenopsis*, the so-called moth orchid. When I was looking for my first orchids, most experienced growers pointed me to *Phalaenopsis*.

They have no faults I can think of. They bloom for months. So long, in fact, that although I never tire of *Phalaenopsis*'s elegant blossoms, I have known growers to get bored with the same old flowers lingering around the house. When blooms fade, the stem can be cut, and a new flower spike will grow from the old one. Some of the smaller-flowered *Phalaenopsis* species are even scented. Let's pot one up and get it ready for the windowsill.

My taste runs to the smaller, more colorful members of the genus. But that still gives me a wide array of choice. There are about 50 *Phalaenopsis* species. The one pictured on these pages is *P. lueddemanniana.* Phalaenopsises are so common these days that your biggest problem may be not so much where to buy them as where not to buy them. In most mid-sized or large cities, they can be found at garden centers, florist shops and even supermarkets. If you have no nearby orchid supplier, the mail-order houses listed in "Sources" carry a wide selection of phalaenopsises. A word of warning: be wary of supermarket plants unless you know where they have been stored. I've heard of orchids being kept in the cooler, perhaps by ill-informed but well-intentioned shopkeepers whose only previous encounters with orchids were of the boxed and chilled high-school-formal variety. Unfortunately, cooling living orchids all but guarantees they will lose that year's growth, at least.

When buying a plant, look for one with shiny, unblemished leaves and plump roots peeking out of the compost. If the orchid is in spike, it

Your first phalaenopsis, **top,** *can be purchased at almost any greenhouse. Small plants,* **above left,** *cost only a few dollars, but it might be wiser to pay more for mature plants that have already bloomed,* **above right.**

may have anywhere from one to several dozen blooms, depending on the variety. You want clear, unmuddied colors in the flowers and no browning, which means the flowers are near their end. Expect to pay around $20 for a healthy specimen. Anything much less should be suspect; anything more may be unnecessary.

Like any houseplant, your new orchid should be able to remain in its original container. But it will require regular watering and feeding. I water by dunking the plant in a bucket of quarter-strength 30-10-10 houseplant food solution mixed in a three-gallon bucket. This way I cover watering and fertilizing at the same time and don't burn the sensitive orchid roots. A 30-10-10 mixture is recommended because fir bark needs more nitrogen than other potting media. If you don't have any 30-10-10, you can use almost any houseplant fertilizer you have on hand. I usually do this once a week—more if the plant dries quickly in summer. If you notice a whitish sediment forming on the bark, cut back on the fertilizer.

Phals, as they are called, like about 1,000 footcandles of light. This much light gives barely a shadow when you stand in it. East windows are best, then gauze-curtained south and west windows. In north windows, they need supplementary light to bloom best, preferably from fluorescent bulbs.

The humidity in many houses is fine for Phals in the summer months, but during the winter, my house in the Northeast, with its overefficient central heating system, gets bone-dry. A humidistat of some sort is a

How to Calculate Footcandles of Light

Special photographic light meters are needed to give instant readings of footcandles, but you can do it with an ordinary hand-held photo meter or your camera. Set the ASA film speed at 200 and the shutter speed at 1/125 second. Hold a large, white sheet of paper in the proposed plant location so that it gets maximum illumination, and be sure the viewfinder shows nothing but white card through the lens. Adjust the f-stop until a correct exposure registers on the light meter.

The following chart gives you excellent ballpark footcandle readings:

F-STOP	4	5.6	8	11	16	22
FOOTCANDLES	64	125	250	500	1,000	2,000

Beautiful and beguilingly easy to grow: Phalaenopsis Agus Ligo 'TC.'

good device to have in your growing area. It is a small, inexpensive gauge available at most garden centers. You can pretest your growing area for suitability by placing the humidistat where your orchids will stand. If the humidity in your house goes below 40 percent, place the orchids on a pebble tray with water added to raise the moisture level around the plants.

My first windowsill growing area sat above some radiators in a Victorian house. I put a board over the radiators and set a tray on it filled with pebbles that sat in water. The pots stood on the pebbles, their feet dry but on a riverbank, as it were. During the winter, the heat from the radiators evaporated the water quite vigorously and provided a surprising amount of local humidity.

Phals like temperatures ranging from the mid-80s F during the day to the low 60s at night. And, in a pinch, they'll take considerably more at either end of the scale. If I've been growing the plants outside in the summer, I like to leave them there until lower night temperatures—in the high 50s—spark the growth of a flower spike. For stay-at-home orchids, this spark can also be provided by tucking the pot against a cool window at night. The process takes about two weeks.

As it emerges, the new spike looks like a little, pointed green knob breaking out of the side of the plant just above the roots. You will know it's not a root when it continues to grow up instead of down or laterally.

Putting Down New Roots

Eventually, your phalaenopsis will outgrow its original container and require repotting–probably every two or three years. Many growers do not recommend repotting a plant in bloom, although if done properly, the process need not be traumatic for the orchid or overly complicated for the grower.

STEP 1. *Lift the plant out of the original pot, loosening the roots that cling to the inside. Cover the bottom of a four-to-six-inch pot with Styrofoam packing "peanuts."*

STEP 2. *Hold the bare-rooted plant over the pot, being careful not to force any of the roots in. They are perfectly happy to "ramble" over the edges of the pot, and in fact, confining them can be harmful. Drop medium-grade fir bark into the pot until you reach the point where the stem begins.*

STEP 3. *Firm down the bark, and your orchid is potted.*

Keep the orchid in the window without rotating the pot, so that the plant remains oriented in a constant position to the sun, and the flowers will come out straight.

Phalaenopsises bloom from around Christmas to late spring, depending on the species or hybrid mix. While in blossom, the plant can be removed from the window for several weeks without too much harm. This is when I like to display the orchids all over the house. I find that orchids in bloom last a couple of pleasurable weeks, even on a dark side table, before they have to be returned to a sunny position. Left in their growing spot, the flowers can remain for months.

When the blooms fade, cut the spike above the third node from the bottom. The nodes are the bumps along the stem from which flowers and branches emerge. The spike will probably start growing again, and you'll get another, usually smaller, blooming. No wonder Phals are becoming the most popular orchids for amateurs and longtime growers alike.

Repotting should be done at least every two to three years if you want the best performance from your plant. Composts such as fir bark will have broken down by then. To repot, lift the plant out of the container, loosening the roots that cling to the inside of the pot. The orchid's roots are now bare, and it should have four or more thick green leaves. Take an ordinary four-to-six-inch green plastic pot. That should be about the right size for any seedling or mature phalaenopsis you buy. I cover the bottom with Styrofoam packing "peanuts."

The leaves should hang over the sides of the pot without dragging on the ground. But don't put a small plant into a pot that is too large. Let the plant's root system be your guide. Hold the bare-root plant upright over the pot, green side up. The thick, fleshy roots should hang inside the pot. If they don't, do not try to force them in. It is perfectly all right to let some of them ramble over the surface and curl around the pot. On their home turf, *Phalaenopsis* roots like to meander in the open air. Forcing them into the pot has only a limited effect anyway—cramped roots will often grow back out of the potting mixture.

Drop medium-grade fir bark—available off the shelf at most large garden centers—into the pot up to the point where the stem begins. Firm down the bark, and the orchid is potted.

Phals are fast-maturing, as orchids go—only two to three years from seed to flowering, as opposed to seven years for some orchids. If any orchid can be said to be ideal to practice on while you get the feel of orchids, it is *Phalaenopsis*. This short chapter probably contains all the information you need if your ambition stops at keeping a Phal or two on your windowsill. But be warned: orchid growing is an addictive pursuit.

If you are like me or any of the thousands of other orchid enthusiasts, you will find that your first orchid merely whets your curiosity to discover more about this, the most beguiling of plant families.

That first windowsill phalaenopsis may be the beginning of a rewarding lifetime hobby.

***Orchids can be perfectly at home anywhere, even on a sunroom floor,* left. *A Phalaenopsis Linda Miller 'Talisman Cove,'* above.**

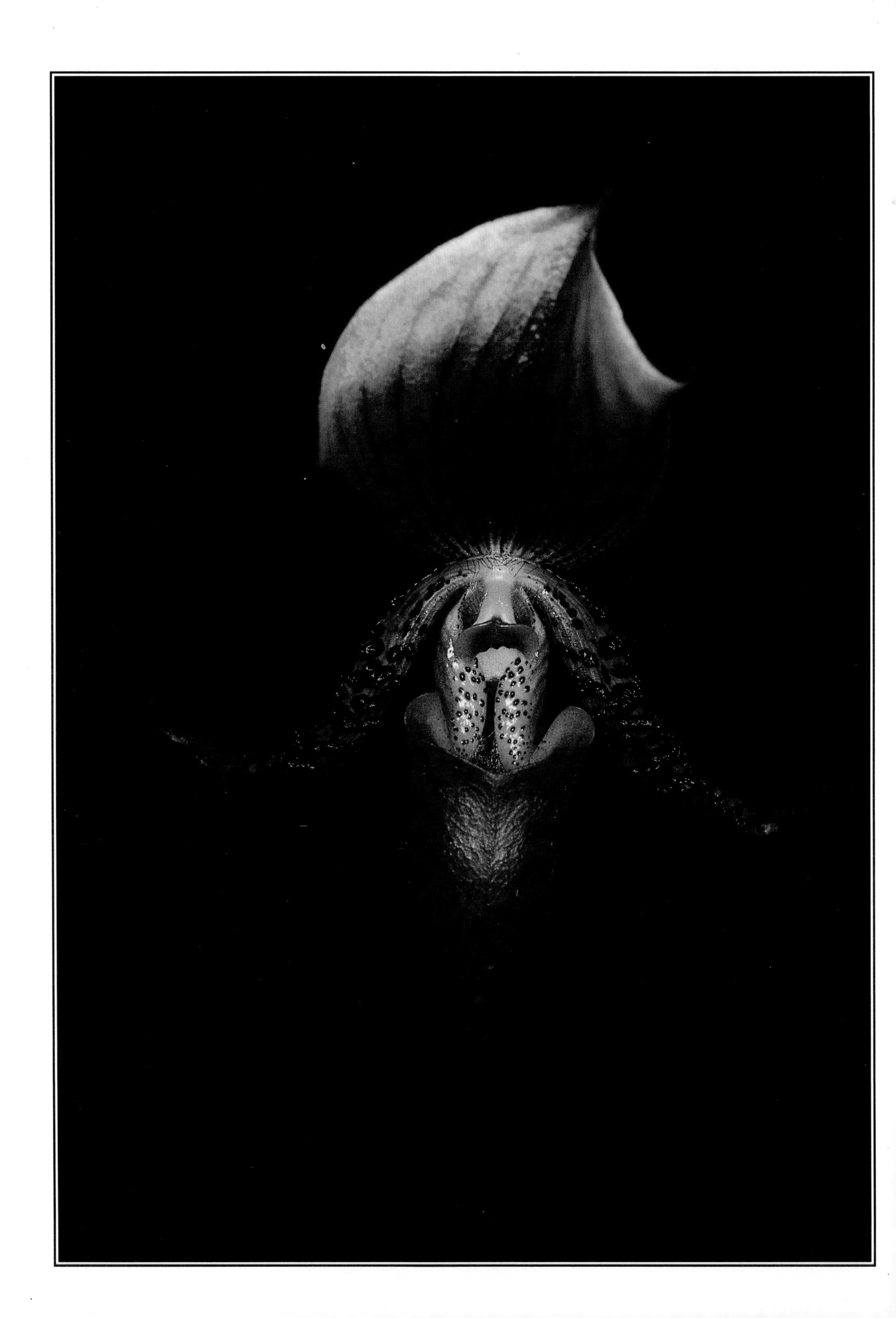

CHAPTER FOUR

Your First Plants

Caveat emptor:
What to buy and where to find it.

I STILL HAVE my first orchid. It was sold to me as *Epidendrum fragrans* by an old-time local orchid grower who probably didn't know what he was starting when he took me round his below-ground greenhouse. I was at that stage in my orchid obsession where I had to see how orchids grow—all kinds of orchids, particularly those I hadn't seen before.

At the time, I was making a habit of calling experienced growers and begging an invitation to see their operations, whether under lights or in greenhouses. The idea was that I would look and perhaps buy their extras.

So I found myself walking between cramped aisles of bewildering variety on that cold and gloomy January morning. Ordinary plants had not prepared me for the different shapes in which orchids display their charms. My eyes couldn't devour the scene fast enough.

It can't have been a very big greenhouse, but I remember it felt like an Aladdin's cavern of treasures. Cascading over the aisles was a jumble of fabulous shapes and colors. Instead of the diminished grandeur of pictures in a book, I was looking at fully developed specimens of *Dendrobium nobile,* with hundreds of white, purple-throated flowers growing out of the sides of two-foot-long stems. There seemed to be entire benches of grotesquely shaped paphiopedilums in combinations of purple, green and blood-red dots with hairs growing out of them, like those on the warts of picture-book witches.

Epidendrum fragrans,* above. Opposite, *an exotic but accessible paphiopedilum.

That's when I spotted my *Epidendrum fragrans.* "Here's something you might try," said Walter. "It's easy enough."

Those fateful words introduced me to a plant that blooms every year and has been grown all over the house at various times, refusing to die no matter what

I do to it. I've divided it into pieces that I've distributed to friends. Even the rankest amateur seems to be able to grow *Epidendrum fragrans*. It's the kind of ego plant every collection needs. It sustains my fascination for orchids even when enthusiasm fades under the onslaught of an especially bad bout of growing—or life.

I was lucky enough to have my epidendrum to get me through the bad spells when nothing seemed to grow, no matter what I tried. This is the kind of plant you should be looking for when you start growing orchids. Ask other growers. Pester the most knowledgeable people at your local nursery. What worked for them? What can't they seem to kill?

Such advice is necessary because the beginning orchidist faces what at first seems like a bewildering number of choices. Not only what to buy but where to buy it and how to find the sources. How do you make sense out of all those Latin names? How do you read plant labels, and how do you remember all the names and classifications of those orchids you've been admiring from afar?

First, let's deal with those tongue-twisting names. The orchids you buy will be either species or hybrids. Species always have two Latin names. The first is the genus and is capitalized. The second, in lowercase, is the species and describes a color or characteristic or is the name of a person. A third Latin name is sometimes added to indicate a "variety."

With hybrids, you will often see a shortened version of the genus name (*Phal.* for *Phalaenopsis*, *Cat.* or *C.* for *Cattleya*) followed by a capitalized word, which is not necessarily Latin. Sometimes, there is additional information, so the label may read something like this: *Blc.* Cadmium Gold (Cadmium Light 'Sweet Lime' AM/AOS x *B. digbyana*). This label tells me that the hybrid is called *Brassolaeliocattleya* (*Blc.*) Cadmium Gold and that it has not received any awards from orchid society competitions. But it has been created by crossing an awarded plant, *Brassolaeliocattleya* Cadmium Light 'Sweet Lime' (hence the AM/AOS, which stands for Award of Merit, American Orchid Society), with a species called *Brassavola digbyana*. When you've read a few orchid books, your tongue will gloss over these terms and names as though you had used them all your life. Trust me, and don't be embarrassed by your temporary ignorance.

What's in a Name?

***O**rchids are either species or hybrids. An orchid species is identified by two Latin terms, both italicized. The first designates the genus and is capitalized. The second, in lowercase, is often a descriptive term, like* Cattleya violacea, *for the violet color of the flowers, or a Latinized variant of the discoverer's name, as in* Cattleya skinneri, *for the great orchid collector George Ure Skinner.*

TWO SPECIES *names linked by an "x," as in* **Oncidium flexuosum x Oncidium ampliatum,** *means the two species were crossed to produce a hybrid. Sometimes, the name of the plant is followed by the name of the parents, in single quotation marks and capitalized. The name is often followed by an award designation, like AM/AOS, which indicates that one of the parents of the cross was declared a superior plant by judges of the American Orchid Society.*

SUPERIOR EXAMPLES *of crosses often receive cultivar names. No other plant may carry this name. So an orchid labeled* Slc. *Vallezac 'Billy Miles' AM/AOS, for instance, will be an exact copy of the orange/red flowers that won the award.*

Your choice of orchids will depend a lot on how greedy your eyes get. On the day I bought my trusty epidendrum, I really lusted after some of the huge cattleyas I had seen in pictures or the *Phragmipedium Grande*, whose petals can measure more than a foot and a half. Like many beginners, I had been seduced by lovely photographs in books. Choosing your first orchid should instead depend on where you live. Your ambient climate

will dictate humidity in winter and summer. How much drying heat must be applied in winter to keep your plant at a happy 70 degrees F? If the answer is "a lot," then you should forget the picture books and think of plants that thrive in the warmer intermediate temperature range.

Fortunately, this range contains

After you master your first orchids, the varieties to choose from become almost limitless. **Clockwise from above:** *An Odontoglossum hybrid, Laelia anceps, Phragmipedium Grande 'Beau Geste' and Masdevallia Angel Frost.*

Phalaenopsis, such as this hybrid, **above,** *and Cattleya,* **opposite,** *are two genera that beginners have little trouble growing.*

some of the most popular orchids grown. It is also the range that makes logical sense for us to explore as we wade toward deeper, more mysterious shoals of orchid growing. It is not necessarily the best range, mind you, since beautiful orchids grow in a wide variety of temperatures and humidities. But it is just so much easier to start at this level.

There does seem to be one common trait among successful orchid growers, however: They eventually specialize in species or hybrids that enjoy a similar climate and concentrate on getting their conditions just right, so that all the plants they cultivate enjoy living together.

If they are fond of cool-growing odontoglossums, say, their growing areas will be moist and cool, with plenty of air movement and an exhilarating buoyancy in the air around their orchids. The plants will be dripping and will have long, hanging, green-tipped roots. In a dimmer cor-

ner, masdevallias will be displaying their chilly flowers in pots with foliage no higher than a croquet lawn. Stately laelias from the brisker mountain slopes of Brazil will grace the benches, and huge cymbidiums will guard the entrance. These species all thrive in mountain conditions in different parts of the world but are perfectly happy together.

Most of us don't tackle the problems of first orchids until we have already bought a few. We buy what we like the look of, and only later do we try to find out whether they can all be grown together. I can remember when my joy over the appearance of a first flower spike turned to consternation as the spike grew and grew, lodging among the fluorescent bulbs under which the plant was perfectly happy to grow but not the flowers themselves. I eventually got the unfried portion of the spike to bloom after rigging a Rube Goldberg contraption of guy lines to hold the spike away from the lights. The orchid lost all its natural elegance, although I got a few flowers. That is not the way to go. But I did learn that size, too, is a consideration when selecting orchids.

You won't go wrong by choosing initially from *Phalaenopsis, Paphiopedilum* or *Cattleya.* Species of *Phalaenopsis* and *Paphiopedilum* are often combined in mixed collections. Both groups are about the same size and can be grown within the bounds of a six-inch pot.

Pronunciation Basics

Angraecum............an-GRYE-kum
Cattleya.................KAT-lee-a
Coelogyne..............see-LOJ-in-ee
Cycnoches.............SIK-no-keez
Cymbidium...........sim-BID-ee-um
Dendrobium...........den-DROH-bee-um
Paphiopedilum.......paf-ee-oh-PED-i-lum
Phalaenopsis..........fal-en-OP-sis
Phragmipedium.......frag-mi-PEE-dee-um

Cattleyas can be a bit difficult. So-called standard, many bifoliate cattleyas are too big. My *Cattleya leopoldii*, stands almost four feet high when it blooms around Christmastime, with about a dozen three-to-four-inch leopard-spotted green flowers. I love it, but as they say in the real estate business, it's hard to place. It lives in the greenhouse.

There are, however, a number of smaller *Cattleya* species and hybrids that make ideal houseplants. Many are prizewinning mericlones—exact genetic copies—of plants whose flowers are superior to the norm. In my collection, my favorite among these little cattleyas is *Sophrolaeliocattleya* (usually shortened to *Slc.*) Jewel Box 'Black Magic' AM/AOS. It's a relatively old mericlone and already has a number of children and grandchildren. But it carries at least four deep red velvet blooms on a plant that is less than a foot high in its pot. The redness is a particular tone that attracts the eye as soon as you walk into the room. And it grows happily on my windowsill.

Mericloning has been a healthy development for the hobby of orchid growing. There are many plants as good as my 'Black Magic,' and each grower has his or her favorites. Again, the secret to finding them is to ask

Full-sized cattleyas can become too large for most indoor spaces, but small cattleyas, such as Slc. Jewel Box 'Black Magic,'* below, *make ideal houseplants.

around. You can often buy them from other hobbyists for $10 to $20 because, since many grow easily and well, pieces of the original plant have been potted up and passed on.

Paphiopedilums have an odd place in the rank of easiest-to-grow orchids. They are among the longest-lasting orchids, appearing to be freshly blooming after months. Despite such desirable characteristics, Paphs are frequently ignored by beginning orchidists. However, many growers who have been at the hobby for a while choose Paphs as their life's work, as it were. Paphiopedilums continue to resist meristem propagation and are often mean in their seed production. So prized plants remain just that, worth a great deal in status—and money, of course—to some growers.

Many of the species Paphs are happy bloomers, and the Indian species are the best in this regard. I grow *Paphiopedilum fairieanum*, *P. hirsutissimum*, *P. insigne* and *P. spiceranum*. They can each usually be had for under $20 and can be grown in about the same light as your *Phalaenopsis* plants but cooler, say, down to 55 degrees F minimum at night.

If you are in an area with temperate summers, like the northern states or southern Canada, Paphs prefer to be outside in summer, and a moist shaded position near the ground suits them perfectly, because that is how they grow in nature.

Even when you have settled on a favorite variety, the simple mechanics of going out to purchase that first orchid can be intimidating. Orchids aren't as rare as they once were, but if you are a beginner, finding the plants you want can still be a formidable hurdle. One good starting point is the yearly catalogs published by commercial growers. They come with price lists and often include growing information. The catalogs included in the "Sources" chapter of this book are excellent resource materials and often have pictures of specific plants, flowering times and temperature classifications. They are sometimes free of charge. In the early years, when I was trying to link names to orchids I saw and liked, I would pore over commercial growers' colorful publications, learning what orchids were supposed to look like long before I saw the real thing.

Of course, if you have the chance, nothing beats visiting commercial ranges, where you can make your selections personally with the help of knowledgeable owners or their staff. These small growers probably started out as hobbyists and just got ahead of

Test Tube Orchids

Mericlone, or meristem, propagation caused a revolution in the orchid world back in 1960, when Georges Morel, a scientist at the National Institute of Agricultural Research in Versailles, discovered a way to produce thousands of genetic copies of individual orchids. Prized orchids could be duplicated exactly. Not all species at first, but other scientists unraveled the mysteries in their labs.

SOON, ***the distinction of owning a true "one-of-a-kind" plant began to disappear. Imagine: Plants that once cost hundreds of dollars a division could now be produced in a lab by slicing up living tissue from the mother plant. There was no limit to the number of copies that could be made. The price of good orchids went down for amateur growers.***

BUT THIS ***hasn't dulled the competition of creating new hybrids. Hundreds are registered every month and placed in a stud book which rivals that for horses in its detail. Most growers balance their collections with both mericlones and various hybrids, hoping for the one plant that will take the orchid world by storm. A popular award winner is worth thousands of dollars in stud fees to go under the scalpel.***

themselves. There are many of them all over the country. When I travelled as a reporter, I often looked them up in the local telephone book and visited their operations. I'd begin by checking for listings under "Orchids" and then move to "Greenhouses." I found many small operations in out-of-the-way places all over the continental United States and Canada. Call before you go.

When buying your first orchids, nothing beats a visit to a commercial range.

If you want to be more efficient, join the American Orchid Society, with headquarters at 6000 South Olive Avenue, West Palm Beach, Florida 33405. The annual membership fee of $30 for U.S. residents ($36 for nonresidents) includes the *AOS Almanac*, which lists affiliated societies and contains a directory of commercial growers. As well, members receive an excellent monthly magazine, in which many of the largest orchid firms advertise with monthly specials.

What can you expect when you send for mail-order orchids from some of these firms? Ads always mention pot size, which is an indicator of the age of certain orchids. An awarded cattleya in a two-inch pot can be had for $15. But it is only a seedling with four years to go before it flowers; then it may be sold for up to $50 in a four-to-five-inch pot. On the other hand, some miniature cattleyas are mature in three-inch pots. The ads usually indicate how long until flowering.

Many species plants are also mature in small pots. So expect to pay $30 for a masdevallia in a two-inch pot. *Phalaenopsis* is sold by leaf span; therefore, something eight inches across and priced between $15 and $20 can be considered blooming size.

Mail order is one of the best ways to acquire new orchids. Unless you specify otherwise, the plants are usually sent "bare root," in a plastic bag surrounded by moss. If you can afford the extra cost of a heavier parcel, have the plants sent in a pot. Many orchids resent repotting and can take a year or two to get back to normal after the trauma of having their roots ripped out of a pot. Most growers will send plants either way.

It is often best to buy plants by mail order from climates similar to your own. The orchids will already have become acclimatized to something close to your environment and will suffer less stress when you bring them into your home.

Also, treat them gently when they arrive. They will have spent up to a week in a dark box, so break their dormancy lovingly. Water them first and put them in a more shaded place than their eventual home. Spray them with water, as well, to encourage the leaves. In a week, they will be ready for their final home. A list of some of the largest growers around the country appears in the "Sources" chapter.

Another question commonly asked is, Do you have to be a millionaire to grow orchids? How much *do* orchids cost? Orchid lore abounds with stories of lost orchids for which vast sums have been paid. One European nursery in the 19th century offered £10,000, then a fortune, for the rediscovery of *Paphiopedilum fairieanum*. Professional plant collectors had picked every known specimen. It was a number of years before *P. fairieanum* reappeared in cultivation after someone discovered a new patch.

Today, I grow one. It cost me only $5, and I look forward in late winter to its oddly colored helmeted flower of old parchment dotted with purple.

If you are able to attend the meetings of orchid societies, there is usually a table where members offer their

Mail order is an easy way to buy orchids. **Above,** *Phalaenopsis seedlings are being packed for shipping.* **Below,** *an order arrives at a grower's home.*

extras for sale. These are some of the best orchid bargains. I bought many of my first orchids this way and experimented with different varieties, depending on what was on the sales table. You can still buy plants for as little as $5 at these meetings and get some friendly advice at the same time. You take your chances with the condition of the plants, though.

In general terms, an ideal orchid will have a rounded, flat flower of large size for its type, with strong, clear colors and texture, which is a quality of flowers that permits them to last a long time. Of course, you can judge these qualities only if you buy the orchid in bloom. Unbloomed seedlings are more of a gamble, but you can afford more of them for the same price. You can even arrange to have orchid nurseries send you a blooming plant each month so that there's always something on the windowsill.

Orchids are valued on a sliding scale, determined by rarity, size, color and flower shape. Awarded orchids are measured and graded on a point scale, so if you buy a plant with a name that ends with AM/AOS (Award of Merit) or FCC/AOS (First-Class Certificate), you are pretty certain of getting a plant with superior lineage.

Once you are on friendly terms with some of the easier orchids, you will be confident enough to try others. There is such a variety of pleasures in orchids that as you collect more, you will find your taste will change. You will begin to admire certain kinds of orchids over others. Perhaps, like Sir Jeremiah Coleman, a famous collector and namesake of orchids, you will grow only rare blue orchids. Or your entire collection of hundreds of tiny botanical orchids will fit on a tabletop. Or, more modestly, you may just look forward to the yearly flowering of a favorite plant. Whatever your pleasure, the best advice is to start with vigorous, inexpensive mature plants that can exist in the conditions you have created for them. After that, the sky's the limit.

CHAPTER FIVE

A Place to Grow

Let there be light, but not too much.

RHIZANTHELLA GARDNERI, an Australian orchid, grows completely underground except the tips of the pale petals, which break a tiny hole in the soil surface for pollination by methods unknown. In nature, orchids are found growing on every sort of surface, from stones to each other. They can break tree limbs with the sheer weight of their numbers, tangible proof of an inherent ruggedness in this family.

Little wonder, then, that among hobbyists, they survive—and often prosper—in the oddest places. Many growers start by keeping orchids in their bathrooms, reasoning that daily showers will make the plants happy. I've seen orchids in apartment closets and, in the right climate, even nailed to front-yard trees. Most of us, however, have few choices about where we grow our first orchids. They are usually placed casually with the other houseplants on windowsills or under fluorescent lights. Doing just this much can be successful for a while, but eventually, the hot, dry air and low light in most homes begin to take their toll. After watching once healthy, plump plants become leathery, flowerless shells of their old selves, I realized why hobbyists have developed inventive solutions to deal with the two biggest problems of satisfactory orchid growing: humidity and light.

***A subterranean Rhizanthella gardneri*, above. *A contented cymbidium*, opposite.**

Central heating is hell on orchids, and even before its introduction, the Wardian case was invented to compensate for the drying effects of coal and wood fires. This is a stuffy Victorian name for an enclosed box with a glass front, sides and/or top. At the height of Wardian cases' favor in the last century, glaziers constructed elaborate room greenhouses on pedestals that did a pretty good

Breathing Easy

There are several ways to raise the humidity around your plants. If plants are short and in small pots four to eight inches in diameter, it is best to set them on wet gravel in shallow trays. If you have taller plants, like cattleyas and dendrobiums, a combination of standing on wet gravel trays with a small fogging humidifier playing over the upper leaves works like a charm.

SIMPLY *keeping your orchids humid is not enough, though. Air movement is a key element in preventing the plants from catching a fungus disease. Preventive medicine is by far the best route to go with your plants. As I write this, there have been tragic consequences for many orchidophiles who have been using a well-known, previously recommended fungicide, Benlate DF. Complaints began to come in to the manufacturer that orchids were stunted and dying. A once benevolent chemical turned rogue. Many of the diseases Benlate was used to treat, however, are preventable with good growing practices, such as adding plenty of air to your plants when you water.*

ON A WINDOWSILL *or under fluorescent lights, low-power desk fans work well in moving the air around without defeating the exercise by driving out the humidity. The secret is in directing the air against the window, for instance, so that the light breeze does not constantly blow on the plants. Good air movement serves several functions. It prevents the air from layering around the plants and forming stagnant pockets, and it brings fresh carbon dioxide to the leaves, helping the photosynthetic process. In my greenhouse, I have found that a Casablanca-style fan works best in moving the air because, at the flick of a switch, it brings cool air from the ground up or pushes hot air down to the ground. It's not surprising that this is the fan of choice in hot countries where human and plant comfort have been refined. It would be good for sunrooms or enclosed patios.*

job of imitating their outdoor manifestation, the glasshouse.

Humidity is retained in a Wardian case, as in a terrarium. With fluorescent lights installed above, small fans inside and a heating cable to warm the atmosphere, you can create a home that some orchids can't distinguish from their own natural environment. Wardian cases are being produced commercially again. Custom-fitted models advertised in orchid magazines can cost from five hundred to thousands of dollars.

Of course, you don't have to spend thousands to get those conditions in your living room. Growers have used old refrigeration cases, and I've seen florists' coolers adapted for living room use. One of the simplest ways of achieving the Wardian case effect is to put your potted plants in a large aquarium in front of a window and under fluorescents. Place a piece of glass over the top, with a space left for air to get in, and it can become a happy home for a number of orchids, particularly terrestrials like paphiopedilums.

Another excellent invention is the greenhouse window. It is like a little lean-to greenhouse, or bay, attached to the space in the wall where a regular double-hung window would be fitted. I inherited one of these on the rear northeast corner of my house, to light a dark wood-paneled kitchen. I'm sure when they installed it, the previous owners did not have orchids in mind. It doesn't have vents that can be opened on hot sunny days, which occur even in late winter in my area. This is a drawback for orchids, but with a little experimentation, I have adapted it to grow plants.

I did this by placing clear plastic over most of the opening to retain humidity and fans on the floor to circulate the air inside the enclosure. With humidity trays filled with pebbles and water and a little greenhouse shading cloth on the outside, the space has become a favorite area to maintain and display orchids.

All orchids left in the open on windowsills or in sunrooms should be placed on grates or stones in trays of water, so that the pots don't actually sit in water. Many garden stores now sell humidity trays that fit window ledges. Sitting in water would kill the all-important roots. Your orchids should also be sprayed daily with water from an atomizer. I have a hand-held plastic sprayer and make it a point to use up all the water in it every time I spray. This makes me feel virtuous about my spraying habits. The spraying should be done by midafternoon to prevent the onset of fungal diseases harbored by foliage that stays wet at night.

Mist humidifiers are a real boon to orchid growers. The old turning-wheel room humidifiers were unwieldy and would become stinky and clogged with calcium and salts from my local water, but the mist models can be placed near the plants, raining sweet mist on them constantly. But don't overdo the moisture. Many orchids, like humans, are happy with humidity levels around 40 to 60 percent.

If you are growing orchids on a sun porch or in any separate room or even outside, one of the handiest devices to have is a minimum/maximum thermometer. It registers how hot or cold it has been since the last setting, so you can get an exact record of temperature variations during a 24-hour period. It is an excellent early alert, especially for gardeners who haven't noticed the season's relentless creep or who want to check how cold it gets in a particular spot in anticipation of putting their plants there. Minimum/maximum thermometers can be purchased for about $25 at major garden centers.

The Wardian case, **above,** *was designed to retain humidity, but a water-filled pebble tray,* **below,** *can accomplish the same goal.*

Another thing to keep in mind is that the orchids you buy were probably reared in a greenhouse under ideal conditions, then sold to a garden center where they received less-than-perfect attention. If the plants have come any distance, like from Hawaii, it may take them a while to adapt to your windowsill. Don't despair; it can be done.

There's an aesthetic danger in allowing the orchids around your window to turn into a jungle of clutter as your collection increases. So if you've absolutely run out of space for your orchids, it's time to think about growing some of them under lights.

Like most newcomers, I had to overcome a psychological barrier when I first began growing orchids under lights. Sure, I had started seedlings for the garden under lights, and I had revived a few houseplants left too long without enough light. But could fluorescent lights maintain orchid plants and make them prosper? There's a suspicion that this is not the way these free-spirited plants are meant to be grown. Yet some of the most successful orchidists practice their hobby exclusively in climate-controlled rooms under artificial lights, where their orchids get exactly what they want and consequently grow and bloom profusely.

The automation that goes with growing under lights makes caring for orchids a less frantic exercise. Even chores like watering and misting can be handled by electrical switches. Given enough ingenuity, orchids can grow easily in an apartment where one room is devoted to nothing but plants under lights. More simply, many hobbyists grow them on plant carts or under light units they've cobbled together themselves.

My first under-lights setup was in an underground room, like a cold cellar, where I nailed together benches and grew some of my earliest orchids. With not much money but plenty of enthusiasm, I visited a wrecker's and, for $60, came away with five enclosed metal six-bulb fluorescent units salvaged from a demolished office building. I bought the six-bulb units because that was all I could get at the time. Many of the orchids would have done just as well under four bulbs.

I suspended the light units from a bar so that I could vary the light intensity by simply moving the bar up and down. I put a plywood bench three feet below the bar. The lights were kept about six inches above the tops of the orchid leaves. I used a three-of-each combination of inexpensive cold and warm fluorescents. You can also add a couple of the special pink-tinged horticultural fluorescents to give your plants a broader light spectrum, as

Functional and economical, a homemade fluorescent light stand, **above,** *makes an ideal growing area for certain orchids.* **Right,** *two minimum/maximum thermometers.*

some authorities suggest. There are many expensive variations of these horticultural growing bulbs. However, many orchids will bloom happily under regular hardware fluorescents.

Tropical light lasts about 12 hours a day, because of the proximity to the Equator, so set your automatic timer for 12 to 14 hours of light. There are orchids, like some cattleyas, that are extremely day-length sensitive. Anything longer or shorter than the 12-hour ideal, and these plants may not flower. All orchids need some rest from photosynthesis. As with humans, important functions take place in the absence of light.

I grew some of my most interesting and exotic orchids under those jerry-rigged lights. Insufficient light is the biggest growth-limiting factor in indoor culture, so when I was able to give my plants a standard 14 hours of light a day, they were in heaven. Some orchids are particularly suited to life under lights. The *Catasetum* family, for instance, grows beautifully in Florida greenhouses, but not in my own. Under lights and at a warmer temperature, I've had them rival those I once saw on fenceposts in the Costa Rican highlands.

Some orchids require more light than can be provided by a simple bank of four fluorescents. This includes members of the *Vanda* and *Cymbidium* families and some *Oncidium* species. For these, you can try growing under so-called very high output fluorescents, but you might also consider installing coated metal halides. These bulbs come in 500-watt and 1,000-watt categories and can light up

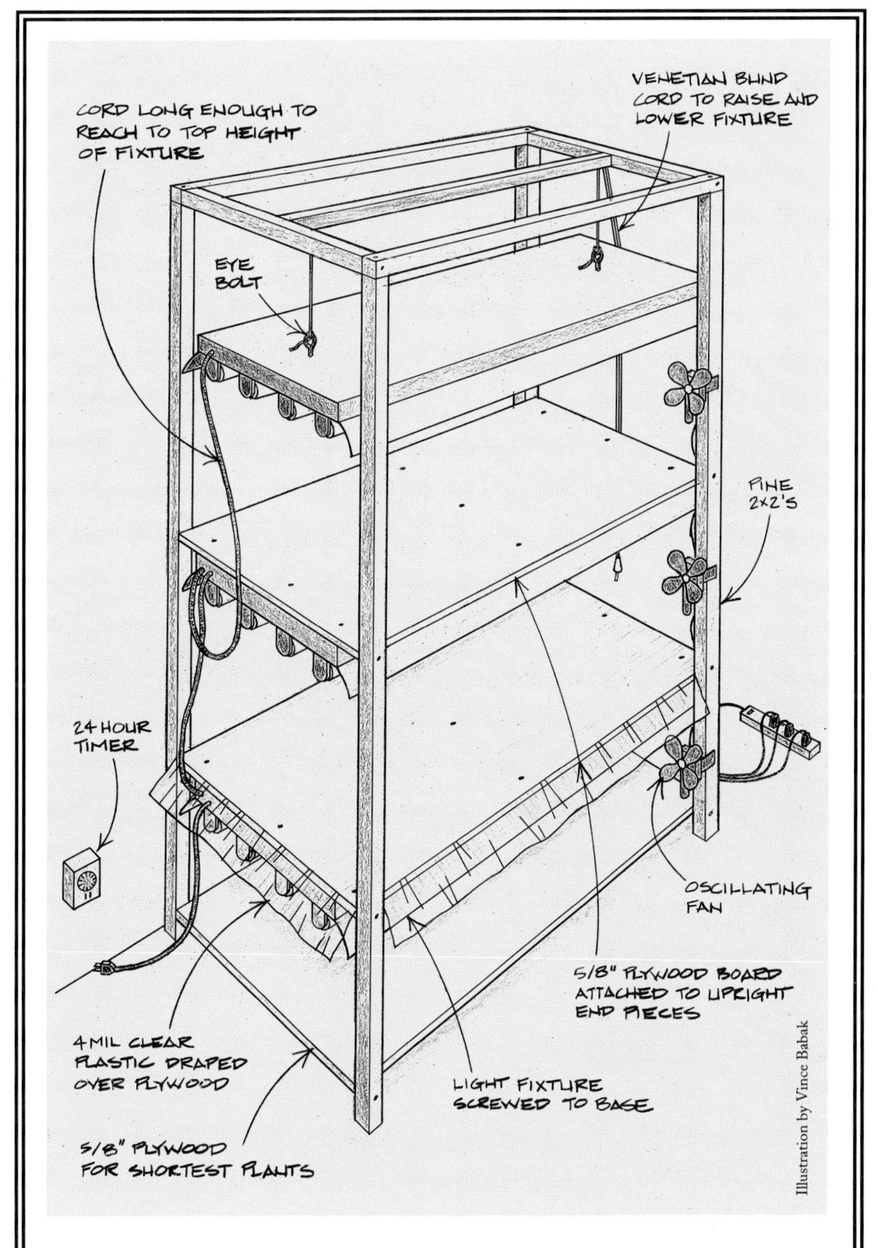

Illustration by Vince Babak

Shedding Light on Your Plants

Light stands with three tiers and fluorescents at each level are manufactured commercially and cost more than $400. A less expensive version can be made with two-by-two-inch and two-by-four-inch lumber and a sheet of half-inch plywood. Forty-eight-inch fluorescent shop fixtures available from lumberyards can be screwed into the plywood. Leave plenty of room on the top tier so that the lights can be moved up and down on ropes. Cover the plywood shelves with thick, clear plastic to prevent water from getting to the wiring. A little overhang of the plastic can be dropped over the front of the lightstand to create a greenhouse-like atmosphere. Fans are important on every level, but they should be small—just enough to move the air briskly. Consolidate the wiring into one cord attached to a heavy-duty electrical timer.

your entire collection, even if it's kept in a basement room. The bulbs are very expensive—up to $150 each.

A good friend of mine has two 1,000-watt lights in his growing room. One is a clear metal halide that covers the blue end of the light spectrum; the other is a high-pressure sodium that covers the red, or harvest, end of the spectrum. Together, they provide more than enough light for any orchid species. There's so much light, in fact, that we don't generally go in unless we're wearing straw hats and sunglasses. A couple of hats hang at the doorway for visitors.

A grow room with this much light presents other problems, like drying out from the high heat generated by the ballasts of these lights. So there's no use trying to grow low-light orchids like Paphs or Phals there, but my friend does have magnificent success with catasetums, oncidiums and cattleyas, whose leaves become spotted with a red pigment, a sure sign that an orchid is at the extreme end of its light preferences. Orchids with thin leaves often bleach to a light green under heavy light.

Orchids under lights generally flower in response to the amount of water given and a temperature differential of from 10 to 20 degrees between day and night. Many dendrobiums, for instance, are made to flower by drying them out in cooler conditions. Withholding water is an important orchid-growing exercise and is usually

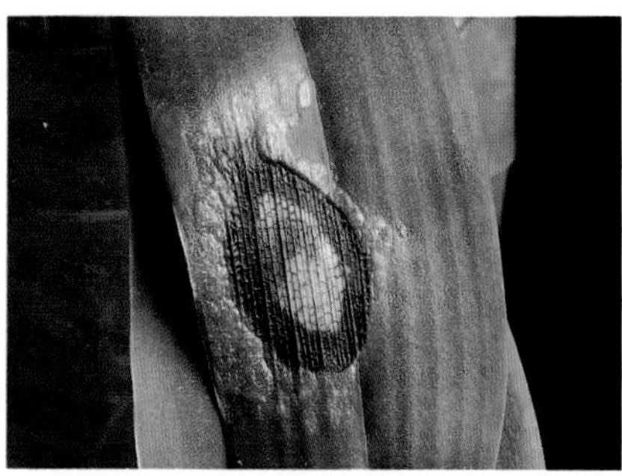

***Some orchids may require high-intensity lights,* left. *Red pigment means this cattleya,* above, *is receiving a lot of light. Sunburned leaf,* top.**

After being liberated from a winter spent inside and under grow lights, this healthy cattleya continues to thrive outside.

done when the plant reaches maturity (when a new growth is fully formed and looks like the one it came from). The drop in night temperature also helps orchids absorb fertilizer and restart the photosynthetic process in the "morning."

While orchids under lights do seem to need more water than those grown "outside," always remember the great cardinal rule of orchid growing: *Don't Overwater*. With epiphytes, unless otherwise indicated, the roots in the compost should be almost dry before being remoistened. There are exceptions, but it's best to try to apply the rule early on in your growing.

Because they grow more quickly, orchids under lights require more food. But as with watering, approach feeding cautiously. Many orchids are light feeders compared with other plants, and if you notice a buildup of whitish residue on the inner rim of the pot or on the roots entering the compost, you are probably overfeeding.

My favorite fertilizer for outdoor feeding or in the greenhouse is the foul-smelling but excellent fish emulsion. It appears to be made of ground-up fish parts rotted to high pungency. But orchid roots love it, and unlike water-soluble chemical fertilizers, fish emulsion leaves no salt residue.

As always, good ventilation is important for orchids under lights. Growers often drape clear plastic over light units to create little greenhouses or line their rooms with plastic so that humidity remains high in the growing area. If they forget to add moving air, it becomes a perfect environment for fungus, a life form even more successful than orchids.

I have to confess a prejudice. Despite their successful application, lights have given orchids a subtly technical aspect that I'm not sure is entirely good. Visiting a serious under-lights grower can be impressive, with healthy plants sporting perfect foliage and large blooms. But it's also like dropping into a hospital. There are electrical cords and hardware everywhere. All those serried rows of plants under garish, unnatural light seem to be happy, but I secretly want them to get well soon, so that they can return to being their flamboyant selves, lolling here and there around the house.

CHAPTER SIX

Potting

Containing your enthusiasm.

ONE OF MY earliest memories of orchids was from a book, a cheap novel for boys, or it could have been a lurid copy of *Boy's Life.* As I remember it, several brave European explorers finally stumble on the remains of an earlier group of adventurers they have been looking for. The skeletons are transfixed with arrows, and the heads are located in a nearby village, hanging in, of course, the headman's compound, with black orchids growing from them. I don't remember the moral lesson the author intended with his tale, but the memory has always comforted me in the knowledge that orchids can grow anywhere.

I'm not sure that skulls haven't been tried as growing containers, but over the years, growers have determined that pots were the easiest receptacle for maintaining an orchid upright in a medium coarse enough to permit plenty of air to the roots. Clay pots were used early and are still favored today by people who grow their orchids in an atmosphere of high humidity and by those who water their plants a lot. Clay, or red terra-cotta, pots encourage excellent root growth because their porous nature allows air at the roots. But since these pots are heavier and more expensive, most orchids are now grown and shipped in plastic pots.

A laelia, **above,** *thrives in the traditional clay pot. Gone-wild roots sprout from an oncidium desperately ready for a new home,* **opposite.**

Because green plastic pots retain moisture around the roots, different growing mixes have been developed to accommodate the orchids. Also, an accidental fall in a plastic pot won't be as critical to the life of the orchid as it would if the plant were in clay.

Early on, after encountering mushy mediums in various kinds of pots, both clay and plastic, I discovered that I was a habitual overwaterer. I couldn't stop fiddling, giving the plants just one more sip. Medium

In dire need of repotting, this phalaenopsis, left, *has severe root damage from sitting in sodden compost. The healthy upper portion of the plant is severed from the rotted roots,* below, *then repotted,* bottom right.

Overwatering caused rot on the center root, top. *Excessive dryness caused the misshapen leaves on the miltonia,* above.

Some orchids are best grown without pots of any sort. This vigorous dendrobium, above, *a native of Indonesia, flourishes tied to a raft of tree fern with a piece of monofilament line, which can be removed when the roots take hold.*

fir bark turned dark brown, then grainy in just a year. Leaves would become yellow and fall off, and pseudobulbs lost their plumpness. Some people mistake such symptoms for lack of water and add even more moisture. Don't.

When I caught this in time, I would take the plant out of the pot and, as often as not, would encounter root rot. Instead of being white and firm, the roots were dark and mushy, with collapsed sides. This is "Condition Red" in orchid growing, and if it isn't stopped, the plant will die.

I clipped the dead roots back, leaving a one- or two-inch fringe to act as an anchor in the new potting medium. Then I left the plant's roots exposed to the open air for at least a day, allowing the rotted area to dry out. I next put the plant in a new pot with fresh medium and secured it with rhizome clips or, if the plant was tall, both stakes and clips either sunk in the medium or clipped to the sides of the pot. The medium was premoistened by being dumped in a bucket with water, so that the tedious process of keeping the medium moist, but not soaking again, could begin. I draped a large open plastic bag over the pot like a tent and placed the plant in more subdued light than it was used to.

If I was lucky and quick enough, the plant still had adequate vigor to initiate new roots and would do so in a couple of weeks. I was often surprised at how greedily the new roots reached out to the fresh medium and brought a seemingly dead plant back to life. Even so, any plant that suffers this indignity will not bounce back right away. Be prepared to lose at least a year's flowering as the orchid struggles to develop a root system strong enough to support it.

My early lack of success taught me that the three elements of pot, potting material and watering are intricately connected. In my case, there was no option but to use plastic pots, and since I knew I overwatered, I had to find a potting material that would be a good compromise between my bad habits and the all-important health

Hints for Potting

REPOT ONLY A FEW *plants at a time.*

DON'T JUMP *from mix to mix. It takes a year to determine how the roots will react to a new potting mix.*

REPOT AT THE END OF FLOWERING, *when new roots appear at the base of the latest growth. Do not let the roots get more than half an inch long before you repot. If roots do get too long, the plant will lose its momentum of growth and often won't flower on the new growth, even if you manage not to break the roots.*

MOST ORCHIDS *begin new growth in the spring. Repot between late winter and early summer.*

IF A PLANT *has to be repotted out of season because of an accident or damaged roots, drape a tent of clear plastic over the plant and pot to retain humidity.*

REPOT INTO SMALLER POT *if the orchid has lost many roots. This makes watering accurately less problematic.*

DON'T DISTURB *an orchid's roots needlessly.*

DON'T LET A PLANT JIGGLE *in its new mix and pot. Secure it with rhizome clips, an upright stick or even masking tape, so that the plant does not move in its pot. An insecure plant is shy about throwing roots and takes forever to reestablish itself.*

Finding a Happy Medium

The most popular potting materials.

CHARCOAL — CORK NUGGETS — CORK SLAB — WINE CORKS

FIR BARK — OSMUNDA — PERLITE — ROCK WOOL

NEW ZEALAND SPHAGNUM — STYROFOAM — TREE FERN — TREE FERN CHUNKS

CHARCOAL: *I use fine grade, which I had to purchase in a bag nearly as tall as I am. This fine grade is apparently used to fuel charcoal heaters but has also been used for years to "sweeten" potting mixes. Helps filter impurities. Lasts forever. Use sparingly. I like a nice sprinkling throughout the mix.*

CORK NUGGETS: *About half an inch around. Excellent for plants that like plenty of drainage, such as bifoliate cattleyas in pots. Usually mixed with bark.*

CORK SLAB: *Good for cattleyas, oncidiums and other plants that like to dry out quickly but spread their roots. Put a pad of New Zealand sphagnum under the plant, then secure it to the bark with monofilament fishing line.*

WINE CORKS: *Excellent for potting vandas in wooden baskets. Plants with thick roots, like species of Vanda, Aerides, Rhynchostylis and Ascocentrum, seem to love curling around this material, no matter what the vintage.*

FIR BARK: *Most popular potting material. Comes in fine, medium and coarse grades. Cheap. Weekly watering.*

OSMUNDA: *The rootball of a fern and the medium of choice for orchids during the last century. Still useful for packing a plant tightly into a pot. Performs best in clay pots by itself. Holds its own weight in water, and roots like growing in it.*

PERLITE: *Heated natural mineral. Looks like small plastic balls. Very light. Popular in peat moss and bark mixes for creating a fluffy texture without waterlogging.*

ROCK WOOL: *Comes in cubes, mats and pellets. Very water-retentive. Can be used alone or as an additive; especially good with bark mix. Fewer insect problems in this medium. Lasts forever but must be flushed regularly to prevent salt buildup.*

NEW ZEALAND SPHAGNUM: *I used to pick local sphagnum from woodland bogs for use as a live growing medium. Must be watered with salt-free water to keep the moss alive. Fantastic for root growth. New Zealand sphagnum has longer fibers. Use alone or in mix where you want to increase water content. Holds thousands of times its weight in water. Good for growing in drier conditions. Do not pack into pot. Phals love this stuff.*

STYROFOAM: *The "peanuts" in packing cases are one of the best bottom layers for plastic pots. Leaves plenty of root room at a spot in the pot where it's useful. Doesn't hold water.*

TREE FERN: *Looks like a jumble of little black sticks. A nice, coarse material for aerating a mix in plastic pots. Comes in a couple of grades: fine and medium, which often seems to have plenty of coarse bits. Also available in chunks, if you really can't leave the watering can alone. Very long-lasting and takes a 10-10-10 fertilizer well.*

For some orchids, such as this Rhynchostylis retusa, wine corks make good potting material.

of the roots of my orchids.

Unlike growers in soil, orchid growers have an almost unlimited new world of potting materials. Once a year, in early spring or late fall, I go leaf collecting in a large public park in the city where I live. I meander through the oak groves, testing the crispness of the leaves underfoot. They must have plenty of texture, and even though they are brown, they must not have started to become part of the humus underneath. I stuff them into a plastic grocery bag. I carry a separate bag for some of the rich, humusy leaves that have begun to decompose. The whole leaves go into a mix I've been using with excellent results to cultivate stanhopeas, orchids whose flowers grow out of any handy hole in the base of the pot or basket. The humusy leaves go into some of my special terrestrial mix.

The Quest for the Perfect Mix is something all keen orchid growers go through and possibly never leave behind. I mentioned in an earlier chapter that repotting an orchid is as easy as dropping it into a pot of fir bark. And it can be that easy, if you want it to be. Over the years, however, orchid growers have tailored mixes to the individual needs of their orchid environments: looser mixes for plants with thick roots; finer mixes for plants with thin, wiry roots; and even no mixes for plants that simply abhor standing water at their roots. Orchid growers use sphagnum moss, cork, osmunda, tree fern, coconut fiber, charcoal, Styrofoam, perlite, vermiculite, rock wool and many kinds of stones and minerals, sometimes all in the same pot.

Some orchid growers believe that new mixes have powerful restorative properties for their orchids. New Zealand sphagnum and rock wool, for instance, are all the rage these

Sprawling unfettered in their native habitat, the thick roots of one species of fox tail orchid firmly anchor the plant to a tree.

days, especially among *Phalaenopsis* growers. Both have an enormous water-holding capacity yet permit plenty of air to reach the roots.

What gardener can resist putting a bit of this and a bit of that together in hopes of creating the perfect mix in which all orchid roots will grow at breakneck speed? Some orchid growers get so excited about such developments, they change over their entire collections to the new mix only to find they have to learn a different way of caring for their plants. Don't get too enthusiastic.

The potting mix I finally came up with is a sort of master mix to which I add different proportions of additional materials I have on hand or decide my plants need at the time. To half a pail of medium fir bark, I add a 16-ounce yogurt container of fine charcoal, a couple of containers of fine fir bark, a container of perlite and, if I want an even more moisture-retaining mixture, another container of New Zealand sphagnum or shredded rock wool. By leaving out the sphagnum or rock wool and adding tree fern, I have a drier mixture for cattleyas. By adding more sphagnum, rock wool or peat moss, I get a fluffier mixture for Paphs or Phals.

The ingredients for your special mix can be obtained at larger garden-supply stores. Many garden centers offer their own mixes. Just remember that once you have chosen a mix, stick with it. Learn to water it properly. Any professional orchid-growing firm in your area will be happy to give you its recipe. Although you don't have to follow it religiously, it's helpful to get an idea of what works best locally. The mix that's popular in New Orleans is not necessarily going to be the best in Connecticut. To maximize the results from any mix, premoisten it so that you don't have to overwater initially just to get the mix into a habitable condition for your orchids' roots.

Watering is a scary concept for the beginning grower. There is a lot of conflicting advice. For instance, the amateur asks the perfectly innocent question, How often should I water? If the question is asked of anyone who has been growing for a while, the beginner will probably get a shifty sort of answer like, "That depends."

This is not the experienced grower trying to be cute or holding back some vital secret from the new grower. In nature, orchids grow on things, so their roots ramble freely, wherever the combination of moisture, food and air works best. When confined in pots, orchid roots—which have an outer layer called velamen that absorbs moisture and oxygen, and a thin, more wiry core—are harmed if they get too much water, or not enough. But it is the "too much" part that usually does the harm. Compost mixes must retain water but not hold it so that no oxygen gets to the roots, which receive even less oxygen if they are housed in plastic pots.

The trick is for your plants to receive only enough water so that they appear to be in need of watering the next day. With organic composts, which break down and therefore retain more or less water depending on their physical condition, the orchid grower is always fine-tuning the watering regime. That's why, for the past century, growers have been trying to grow orchids in inorganic compounds, to sidestep this problem of the breakdown of compost and its toxic effect on the roots.

Whether you choose to grow them inside or outside, orchids such as this phalaenopsis are best watered by immersing the plant, pot and all, in a bucket.

I'm convinced that watering is a learned art form, understood by close observation of your plants and the conditions they favor.

at Bow Bells
Joan Holloway AM/AOS

CHAPTER SEVEN

The Great Outdoors

A summer in the backyard can result in an autumn bounty of blooms.

ORCHIDS are like those inner-city kids you read about who, after being taken out of their normal environment and sent to camp for the summer, come back transformed and healthy, with the best aspects of their personalities suddenly apparent. That's what happens to orchids when they are released from their greenhouses and windowsills and allowed to go outdoors. The effects of natural air circulation, sunshine and rain are nothing short of phenomenal.

After a summer outdoors, orchids that never bloomed before often do, shortly after being brought inside. Their foliage is greener, their bulbs plumper and their dispositions more tolerant of the abuse of a coming winter inside. Outdoor growing is the secret to blooming many terrestrials, and I put out not only orchids but also many leafy houseplants. I'm convinced this is why many of them are still alive after a decade in the same pots.

As winter draws to a close here in Ontario, all my houseplants are at the end of their tether. There's just so long plants can subsist on four hours of light a day, as they often have to in awkward windows. Many orchids won't survive on so little light. But somehow, by being outside for three or four good months, the orchids revive.

Assorted orchids bask in the open air,* above. Opposite, *a cattleya on a patio.

Many orchids can go outside surprisingly early if they are properly sheltered. Of course, I don't just take them all outside one day when the weather gets nice in early May. First, I use my minimum/maximum thermometer to determine how cold it gets at night in the

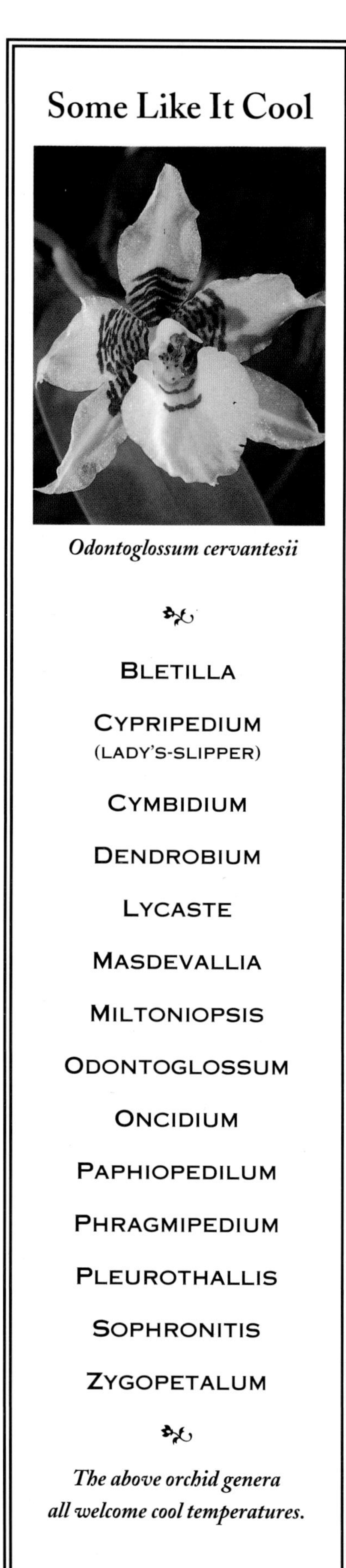

Some Like It Cool

Odontoglossum cervantesii

BLETILLA

CYPRIPEDIUM
(LADY'S-SLIPPER)

CYMBIDIUM

DENDROBIUM

LYCASTE

MASDEVALLIA

MILTONIOPSIS

ODONTOGLOSSUM

ONCIDIUM

PAPHIOPEDILUM

PHRAGMIPEDIUM

PLEUROTHALLIS

SOPHRONITIS

ZYGOPETALUM

The above orchid genera all welcome cool temperatures.

locations I've chosen, because the night temperature is critical to the well-being of some orchids. Don't put any warm growers out until you can plant tomatoes in your garden, and even then, don't push it.

For two years running, I killed the chances of a number of cymbidiums by not protecting them from the elements. Rainwater lodged in the new growths. The plants were happy as long as the sun shone, but when the rain came and a cold spell followed, all the new growths rotted, because I didn't have the presence of mind to keep them under cover. Once I learned to place the early orchids under a sheet of translucent fibreglass, the new growths took off outside, and that winter, those cymbidiums gave me the best blooms I ever had, even in the greenhouse. And there's nothing quite so exotic as having orchids hanging in the patio among the ordinary houseplants.

Orchids can be grown outside for at least part of the summer over most of North America. The trick is learning how to handle the vagaries of locally unpleasant conditions. Some people grow orchids in arid desert regions, but my recommendation is to go to the more humid climate of inside. Many areas in the southeastern United States can accommodate orchids living in trees or lawns for most of the year. Some orchidists in California, Florida and Hawaii can grow them outside year-round, lucky devils. In these areas, orchids can be naturalized on trees by tying them to the limbs or trunk, where they grow as they do in nature. The process is very much like growing orchids on cork rafts. Get some osmunda, New Zealand sphagnum or peat moss, and place a wet pad of it under the roots. Lash the plant to the limb with heavy monofilament fishing line, and water with a hose until established.

In other areas, growers winter their plants under lights and put them out in spring. When these orchids are taken back inside in autumn, they go into the dormant/flowering phases and flower almost immediately. This is particularly true of certain Indian dendrobiums, which are often impossible to bloom if kept inside at a steady temperature all year.

The annual exodus outside allows the grower to give the plants a thorough health inspection after a long winter. It is very easy to lose a plant when it is hidden among the others on the shelf all year. I've had orchids bloom without my knowing it because they were tucked behind other plants. Only in the spring, when it came time for the trip outdoors, did I discover the shrivelled brown flower corpses. The spring airing also provides an ideal opportunity to examine the orchids for pests such as scales, which look like little brown domes on both sides of the leaves; mealybugs, which resemble small cottony masses and are found under the drying sheaths at the base of pseudobulbs; spider

Daily spraying,* top right, *is the key to the health of orchids, such as this phalaenopsis, particularly during warm weather.* Bottom right, *an oncidium flourishes on a lattice fence.

mites; and snails.

If I had to choose one pest from the rogues' gallery that plagues home orchid growers the most, it would be the spider mite. If you notice wispy spiderwebs in the leaf crotches of your orchids or your phalaenopsis leaves suddenly develop tiny pits and begin to look thin or the thinner leaves of your dendrobium take on a silvery sheen, your plants are infested with spider mites. Although difficult to detect with the naked eye, under my $30 hand microscope, they look like translucent spiders cut off at the first joint of their legs. These stubby creatures can do an incredible amount of aesthetic and physical damage to houseplants of all kinds. Unfortunately, by the time they are spotted, they have usually done it.

As the temperature rises and the humidity drops in the plants' growing area, spider mites begin to breed at an astounding rate. They love hot, dry conditions. In a week's time, the precious leaves of your orchids will start to drop, as their juices are sucked away. Don't panic. There are ways to eliminate spider mites. Humidity is the important factor. If that can be kept high, mites can be controlled.

All orchid growers should use a pump-spray bottle of plain water to wet the plants and humidify the air around them every day. Check the minimum/maximum thermometer to see how hot it's been getting in the growing area. Temperatures may soar to more than 90 degrees F during the day, and if there is no moving air, spider mites are encouraged beyond the bounds of modesty. There are special

miticides available, like Kelthane, as well as outdoor sprays, but they solve the problem only temporarily. My policy is to use them once to get rid of the initial infestation, then change the environmental conditions. Fortunately, spider mites are mostly an indoor problem, a pest for enclosed areas like windowsills and greenhouses. Outside, breezes keep them down.

Dry air also encourages scales and mealybugs, which suck the juices of orchids. Raising the humidity will help to control these pests as well.

A number of authorities recommend attacking mealybugs with a cotton swab dipped in rubbing alcohol. I can remember trying this when I was a novice grower. It lasted about five minutes. There I was dabbing and daubing, but I always suspected that I was missing some. They literally dropped off, however, when I switched to a pesticide like diazinon or malathion. Adding a few drops of liquid dishwashing soap to the pesticide solution will make it more effective: the soap dries and stays on the leaves longer, holding the pesticide in place. I don't use horticultural oils on orchids. Now, by applying my blitzkrieg pesticide solution to plants infested with mealybugs and changing the conditions in which my orchids are being grown, I find the problem does not reappear.

Next to spider mites, snails are the worst orchid pests. Many growers

A burgeoning Epidendrum ibaguense on a California patio.

Rogues' Gallery

A guide to common orchid pests.

Fungus Gnats

Tiny gray flies that live in compost which is kept overly wet. Seem to be more annoying than anything else.

Mealybugs

Little cottony masses found under dry sheaths and in leaf junctures in plants under stress because of dryness, dying roots or poor care. Check the roots and move the plant.

Scales

Hard scales look like small brown helmets on leaves or stems; suck plant juices. Soft scales excrete a honeydew that attracts black mold and ants to the orchids. Both easy to control with chemicals and change in humidity.

Snails and Slugs

Feel no guilt. Crush them dead wherever they appear. More common in wetter greenhouse collections, but once lodged in a pot brought into the house, they roam at will at night, nibbling root tips. Control with slug pellets or drench.

Spider Mites

Tiny pinprick holes in leaves, which become spotted with yellow. Spiderwebs. Appear when plants kept in hot environment.

Whiteflies

These rise up in a white cloud when approached. Can occur when orchids are grown in a greenhouse with other plants, like tomatoes.

Building a Lath House

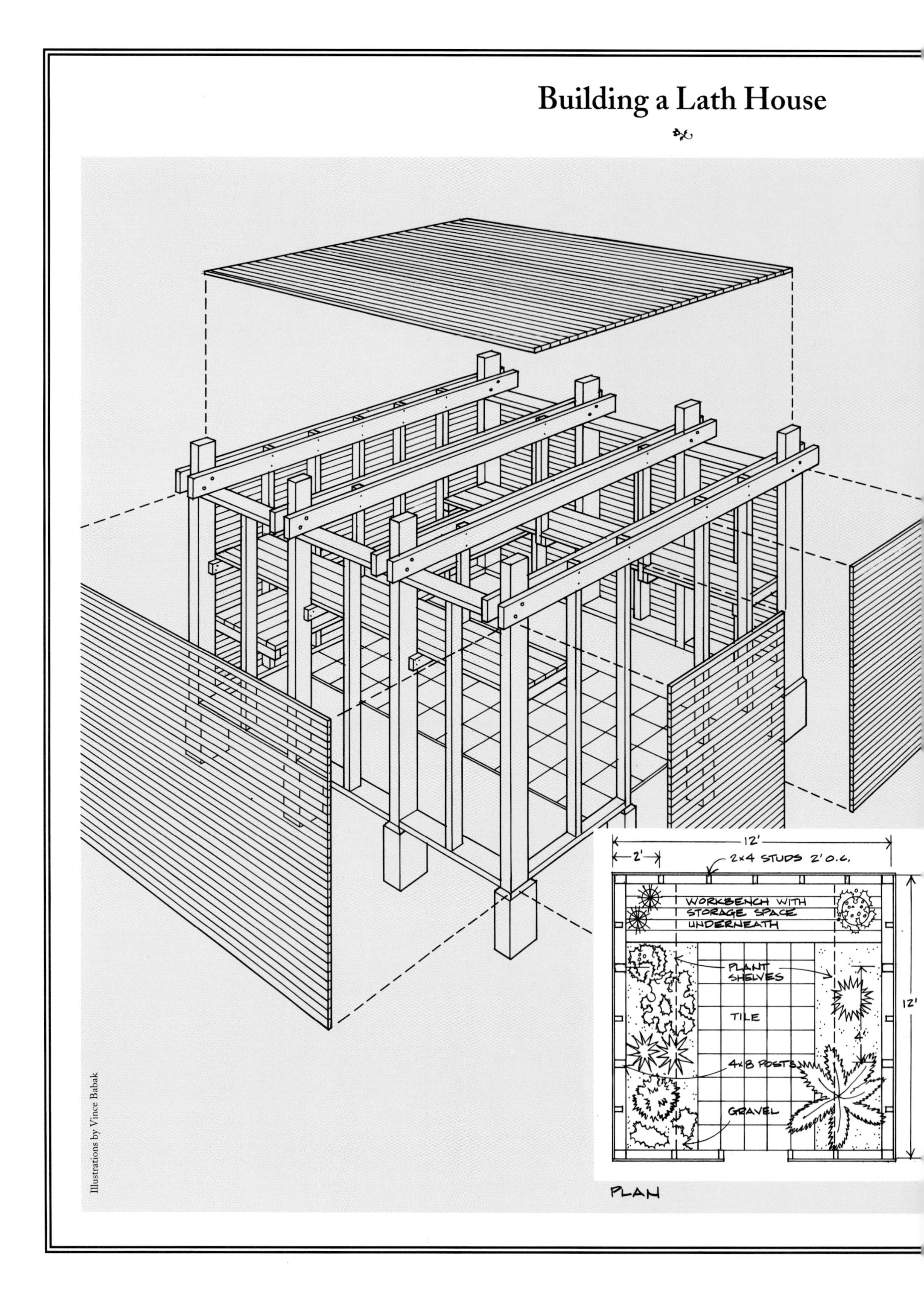

Illustrations by Vince Babak

This is a wonderful structure "to go to" at the bottom of the garden or in a sunny corner. It has the shading of an enclosed greenhouse without the stifling conditions. Orchids can be kept in a lath house for much of three seasons in my part of the world, in the Northeast.

ORCHIDS ***and many other houseplants love to bloom in lath houses. Benches along the walls make the area even more useful, or plants can be hung from the ceiling in the traditional fashion. A simple structure with no wood lathing but with a piece of greenhouse shade cloth draped over it would also work. It's good to have a water tap nearby so that the orchids can be sprayed with a garden hose once a day. I use a fine mister nozzle, available from many garden centers.***

DON'T MAKE ***a lath house too small. You'll need room in there for yourself as well. I recommend a 12-by-12-foot structure, with a gravel floor for the best humidity. Concrete slabs also soak up and hold water, so the orchids receive moist, moving air from underneath. Popular structures in Victorian times, lath houses served as outdoor living rooms, and they deserve as much attention today.***

claim snails *are* the worst. I usually give the title to whichever one I have at the moment. Snails come in various shapes, but those I find most often in my orchid compost have a gray disk-like shell and can be as small as pinheads. But what damage they do to the tips of orchid roots! Simply picking them off is a problem, because they are so hard to see. I've tried slug pellets, powders and drenches, but persistent snails keep coming back. In bad infestations, I've resorted to repotting and discarding the old compost, which probably contains millions of snail eggs.

Stress is a factor in the susceptibility of orchids to disease. Grow them correctly, and disease will stay away. Fungal and bacterial diseases can be cleared up quickly and basically in the same way: a shot of fungicide/bactericide (they can be bought in one solution) and a change in the plants' growing conditions. In the case of fungi, dry up the area where they grow by introducing plenty of moving air.

If I have a bad outbreak of "everything," I sometimes dip the entire plant in a pesticide solution. "Everything" is a condition you find when buying a plant from questionable sources, such as new hobbyists getting rid of their problem plants, or when you have sorely neglected your own plants. This situation can be dealt with by the simple expedient of dipping the entire plant in a drench, a solution of something like malathion in a big bucket of water. After drenching, the plants are hung out to dry in the spring breezes. I try to keep to only one drenching a season for the good of my plants. Think of chemicals as a last resort, and don't use pesticides or fungicides at all unless you absolutely must. There's some question about long-term genetic effects on orchids from the use of too many powerful chemicals.

The word virus strikes fear in the hearts of orchid growers. There are said to be 18 viruses that can affect orchids. Among the most feared are strains of tobacco mosaic and cymbidium viruses as well as a virus derived from beans. The best way to describe the symptoms is to say that orchids infected with viruses just look bad. They are weaker plants that exhibit mosaic patterns on their leaves, often circled by rings of brown, and have streaked flowers.

I once had a mericlone of *Cattleya* Chocolate Drop 'Kodama' AM/AOS. It was the perfect plant, growing about 16 inches high and topped with up to 18 cattleya flowers on a single stem, the petals flushed a deep, rich mahogany red. It had a heavy tropical scent at certain times of the day. I loved that plant when it was in bloom. But one year, the flowers began to get smaller, and I noticed the plant wasn't growing as well as it had in the past.

Then last year, it bloomed again, this time with flowers not only greatly reduced but a dirty, faded mahogany red streaked here and there with darker reds. It probably caught the virus from another plant introduced into my collection. The plant wasn't dying, exactly; it was just deteriorating. Reluctantly, I threw it out.

The dappled light on a porch provides ideal growing conditions for this collection of dendrobiums and cattleyas.

The orchid literature urges growers with apparently virused plants to remove them from the collection. Viruses can be spread by using the same cutting tools on infected and then uninfected plants. If I am doing a lot of plant division, I use one of those handyman propane torches on the blade of my cutting instrument for a few seconds. This is the best way to destroy all viruses, better than the simple bleach solution that is sometimes recommended.

I'm still not sure whether I did the right thing with my Chocolate Drop. It could simply have been poor care that caused the plant to deteriorate or too much fungicide or pesticide applied during an important growing stage. A number of conditions mimic the effects of virus disease. Besides, several orchid paintings from the 19th century show the telltale streaking of virus. So virus has been around a long time among orchid growers. Not all plants die from it. I still ask myself, though, whether I could have saved it. Fortunately, with modern orchid growing, there are more copies of *Cattleya* Chocolate Drop 'Kodama' AM/AOS around, and I can start again.

The American Orchid Society publishes an excellent reference called *Handbook on Orchid Pests and Diseases* ($9), which covers not only all the common bugs that affect orchids, including their mug shots, but also plenty of information on control and the still hazy subject of viral diseases in orchids.

In addition to being a good season for dealing with your plants' health concerns, spring is the ideal time of year to repot, because the best outdoor months are approaching. In the warm weather and rains of spring, orchid roots grow their fastest.

Those are the good points of growing outside. The bad points often include dry weather, too much sun, low humidity, wild animals chewing your plants, sudden storms knocking things over, unexpected frosts and a whole new world of hungry pests.

Some of these problems, however, can be avoided by a careful choice of site. My favorite outdoor growing area is a patio shaded by trees, from whose branches I can hang orchids that receive dappled sunlight most of the day. Cool porches and terraces also work well. From such locations, plants can be closely monitored so that they don't get too much sunlight or too little water, the two most common outdoor horticultural sins. Once they've spent a week or two outside, plants can be moved to selected areas around the garden to suit their needs for more or less sunshine.

One of the best inventions for outdoor plant growing of any kind is the lath house, which is covered with spaced laths so that the moving sun never shines for long on any one part of the leaf, thereby burning it. This simple structure, with its open lath sides, encourages lots of airflow, and watering is a snap. Orchids are admirably suited to lath houses. They are especially useful for growers with no shady areas outside, and city gardeners love lath houses because they work well on flat roofs.

A less costly outside shade area for orchids can be constructed with a simple frame covered in greenhouse shade cloth. Made of a material that looks like the bags onions are packed in, shade cloth, which is black, is available in several densities from greenhouse suppliers. It, too, permits plenty of airflow. I know I'm being a bore about the need for moving air for orchids, but some growers don't realize until years later how many diseases and problems could have been avoided had they simply kept the air moving.

Cool nights can harm some sensitive orchids, including many vandas.

Summer care for orchids is generally just a matter of hosing them down. Many orchids handle heat stress better when kept outside during the summer, especially if given plenty of water. But a careful watch must be kept in late summer, when temperatures begin to drop. The cooler nights initiate blooming in many orchids, and for me, it's usually a race between the weather and my desire to assure my plants get a jolt of coolness. One October, I lost all my *Odontoglossum pendulum* (sometimes called *Odontoglossum citrosmum*) plants because I was experimenting with cold tolerance. Nothing seemed to flower these Mexican orchids, which have pendent sprays of two-to-three-inch flat, white blushed flowers with an extended violet lip and a terrific scent. They bloom in late spring, and my faulty reasoning was that if I gave them a good nip of coldness, they would send out their flower spikes. We had a freak frost, however, and the lot of them were wiped out in one night. That lesson taught me not to tempt nature.

Most members of the *Vanda* family don't like to stay out too late in the year, especially in the more temperate North. These huge tropic-loving Asian natives, with palm-sized flowers, relish a humid lowland languidness. But some species like cool, fresh nights.

On an easy walk in the hills above the lake town of Pokhara, in Nepal, I saw many varieties of orchids, including *Vanda* with small lavender-blue flowers. I was in the foothills of the Himalayas in January, with an excellent view of the Annapurnas, some of the highest mountains in the world. Even warmly dressed, I did not like to be out in these hills on a winter's night, yet the orchids were thriving in the chilly, dew-lapped mountains. That lesson showed me that nature often tempts itself.

CHAPTER EIGHT

Orchids You Can Grow

A sampler of popular species.

LONG BEFORE I understood the mysteries of keeping a few easy-to-grow *Phalaenopsis* plants alive, I began to covet other genera. Could I bloom some of the magnificent specimens I saw in photographs? Frankly, I didn't care what the answer was. I simply had to try some. I ordered plants I couldn't even find in my small collection of reference books.

I remember a Brazilian firm, in particular, that offered 25 orchid species for $25. I applied to the federal government for an import permit, which is necessary when purchasing orchids from other countries. A few weeks later, my plants arrived.

Christmas had nothing on this, my first international order of orchids. I guess I was expecting lush clumps of cattleyas, their flowers still perfectly happy and perky after being shuffled and shunted by a variety of unsympathetic hands and spending weeks in a lightless box. What I got was a mix of large and small plants attached to dried bits of osmunda or tree fern. Many were already dead, although I revived a few, which grew for a couple of years.

That order was a lesson in humility. I learned a lot about reviving desiccated plants, and I also discovered that the world of orchids is so vast that there is room for many more interests than I had imagined before.

Soon, there was no stopping me. The following are some favorite orchid genera I've tried, along with my suggestions about how to grow them successfully:

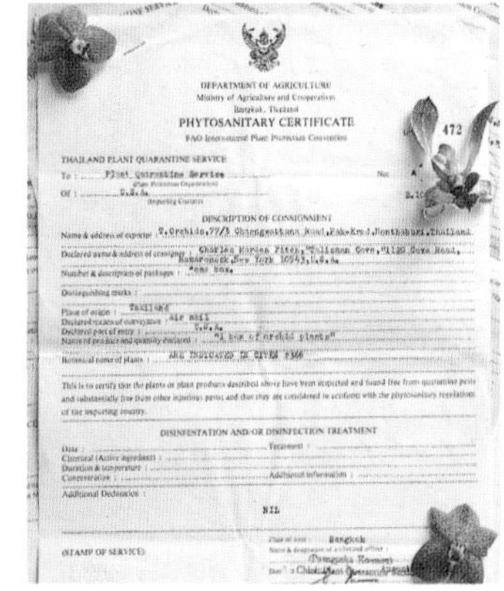

DEPARTMENT OF AGRICULTURE
Ministry of Agriculture and Cooperatives
Bangkok, Thailand
PHYTOSANITARY CERTIFICATE
FAO International Plant Protection Convention

472

THAILAND PLANT QUARANTINE SERVICE

DESCRIPTION OF CONSIGNMENT

Place of origin: Thailand

DISINFESTATION AND/OR DISINFECTION TREATMENT

Additional Declaration: NIL

(STAMP OF SERVICE)

Place of issue: Bangkok

Cattleya bicolor, a summertime bloomer, **opposite.** *Import certificate,* **above.**

CATTLEYA

A survey a few years ago asked members of the American Orchid Society to name their favorite orchid. They chose *Cattleya*, hands down. This is the orchid of the high school prom and the illustrated chocolate box: lush, huge-lipped and floppy. When the fashion world speaks of orchid as a color, it is invariably a lavender shade, like the first cattleyas imported to England from Brazil in 1818. They were named for William Cattley, who rescued and revived several plants that were being used as packing in an order of other tropical species. Or, at least, that's how one story goes. Another has Cattley returning from a plant auction with a sorry-looking specimen that was, in fact, *Cattleya labiata*, the plant upon which the genus is based.

Clockwise from above: *Laelio-cattleya Winter Ruby, the author's Cattleya skinneri, Cattleya Small World, a "minicatt" measuring six inches tall.*

There are about 60 species of cattleyas native to Central and South America. In the wild, they range from the steaming Amazon jungles to the slopes of the Andes, where temperatures drop to near freezing. This is what makes many of them adaptable to a variety of climates. In addition to their adaptability, they are also justly popular because of their large-sized flowers and their relative ease of culture.

Cattleyas are divided into two groups: unifoliate and bifoliate. The unifoliate group has plants that bear one big leaf on a club-shaped pseudobulb. The flowers are usually big and floppy, with large lips. *C. labiata* and *C. trianaei* are common examples.

Plants in the bifoliate group have two leaves and smaller, more compact flowers, but in greater numbers. My *C. skinneri*, for instance, has up to 10 flowers on each pseudobulb. Bifoliates also boast more diverse and interesting colors than unifoliates, ranging through shades of purple, pink, white, yellow, brown and green. Some, like *C. schilleriana*, are richly splashed with tawny spots on green petals, with a lip dominated by violet veining. *C. amethystoglossa*, another bifoliate, has pink flowers with heavier lavender spotting. Good specimens have a lovely charm that points up to their natural exuberance.

Cattleyas can be very sensitive to repotting at the wrong time. This is especially true of some bifoliates that resent even being in pots, like *C. aclandiae*, which I have only been able to grow on cork rafts, and the rarer unifoliates, like *C. dowiana* var. *aurea*.

In a sense, *Cattleya* is a misnomer for this genus because these days, most of the so-called Catts grown by hobbyists are hybrids that meld the genes of not only *Cattleya* but also *Laelia*, *Brassavola*, *Sophronitis*, *Broughtonia* and *Diacrium*, among others. The proclivity of orchids for intergeneric combinations has added to the *Cattleya* family new colors, more flowers and flowers with different shapes from the traditional cattleya of the high school corsage.

For instance, *Brassavola digbyana*, a related orchid that looks like a white cattleya except for a bizarrely fringed and enormous lip, was incorporated

***Cattleya labiata*, the Brazilian species that was responsible for the Cattleya craze which began in the early 19th century.**

early in cattleya hybridizing to increase the size of cattleya lips. The subsequent hybrids were called brassocattleyas. Some of them also inherited the lemony scent of their *B. digbyana* ancestor.

Then species of *Laelia* were bred to brassocattleyas to improve the texture of flowers and add a new range of colors, particularly yellows, oranges and even blues. They became brassolaeliocattleyas (*Blc.* for short) or, if they lacked the *Brassavola* parent, laeliocattleyas (*Lc.*). There are now quadrigeneric and quintigeneric Catts, but I find most of the very complex *Cattleya* hybrids harder to grow and more interesting as curiosities than some of the simpler, primary hybrids. All the extra genes seem to make the plants more finicky about the conditions they will tolerate.

There's no single season when cattleyas flower. Most begin to develop a new pseudobulb in the spring. Some flowers emerge from the green sheath that develops after the leaves have formed. Others develop a sheath, then rest, with nothing happening to the sheath until the following winter. I've also had cattleyas flower with no sheath at all. Blooming times are further complicated when Catts are crossed with other genera. My first *Cattleya*-alliance blooms start around Christmas, and depending on the type and cross, there are periodic flushes of bloom right into summer.

I recommend buying orchids that flower when you will most enjoy them. For instance, I derive the greatest pleasure from my orchids during the winter months, which, in the Northeast, cover three seasons. I get a yearning to acquire new blooming plants in the seasons when my outdoor garden is out of bloom. By acquiring orchids that are in bloom from

autumn to spring, I can hope to bloom them again around the same time the following year and for many years thereafter.

How often do cattleyas flower? By and large, once a year, although they can flower more often. In an ideal tropical climate, they will bloom as each growth matures, no matter what the season. Growers who keep their cattleyas under lights year-round can duplicate this kind of growth, especially with smaller varieties.

Hybridizers have developed various races of "minicatts." These are miniature versions of *Cattleya*, with smaller blooms in the yellow-orange-red range, often with names that contain the word Pixie. They are cattleyas, but they lack the big, flamboyant flowers that endear this genus to so many growers. On the other hand, you can grow more of them on a windowsill.

To perform best, cattleyas need temperatures that range between 55 degrees F at night and up to 90 degrees during the day. They also like bright light and plenty of humidity, with a drop in temperature at night. Because humidity is so difficult to maintain in a windowsill, Catts are really a second choice for this location.

Despite their general ease of culture, some cattleyas won't flower no matter what you do. To avoid this kind of trauma for as long as possible, choose plants that have already bloomed. Look at the older pseudobulbs for signs of flowering. Do the sheaths have bits of old flowering stem still visible? If not, it may be a finicky orchid. Also, if it is mature enough to flower and hasn't yet, it's a good bet this plant is a reluctant bloomer. Choose another. There are thousands of species and hybrids to try. There's no point spending frustrated years trying to bloom an orchid if it won't cooperate. Or at least choose your frustrations carefully. I know, I've been there.

What to grow? You'll be influenced by the orchids you see at nurseries and shows. Tastes vary around the continent, as do the conditions that cattleyas like best. It's sort of a rule of thumb that cattleyas with plenty of *Laelia* in them grow better on the West Coast than they do in Florida or Hawaii, especially if they are cultivated outdoors.

Since cattleyas interbreed readily with other members of the orchid tribe, I've listed some of those members among my favorites, including *Laelia*, *Epidendrum*, *Encyclia*, *Brassavola* and *Diacrium*. Here are a few of the species I like, starting with the true cattleyas:

C. aurantiaca A good specimen of *C. aurantiaca* can have bright orange

Frilly-lipped Brassavola digbyana, **left,** *is the basis for all Brassavola hybrids.* **Top,** *one color variation of Cattleya aurantiaca.* **Above,** *the popular Cattleya forbesii.*

two-inch flowers, a dozen of them on the stem emerging from the bifoliate leaves. This species' genes swim in a vast tidepool of orchid hybrids. It has added its color range and hardiness to many hybrids with cluster flowers. One of my favorites is *C.* Chocolate Drop 'Kodama' AM/AOS, which has a combination of red, chocolate and cream colors and a spicy scent. *C. aurantiaca* likes to grow on the dry side for cattleyas, with plenty of water when the new growth is forming—and plenty of light too. Although it should dry out between waterings, don't use this as an excuse not to water. Keep the pseudobulbs plump with judicious watering. Hybrids of this species are usually ready to go out for the summer, and as a result of the experience, they flower lavishly—mine blooms winter to spring.

A C. Chocolate Drop 'Kodama' with vigorous roots.

CATTLEYA BASICS:
A CHECKLIST

LIGHT: *2,000–3,000 footcandles*

TEMPERATURE: *55° to 90°F*

HUMIDITY: *40 to 80 percent*

FERTILIZER: *Half-strength 30-10-10 during growing period; 10-20-10 before flowering*

WATER: *Alternate wet and dry*

COMPOST: *Fir bark, tree bark, osmunda*

REST: *Two weeks after flowering*

C. bowringiana This is a very Victorian orchid discovered in Honduras in 1884 growing lithophytically (on stones) near a stream. It has an elegant high presence and can carry up to 20 three-inch rose-purple flowers on a bifoliate plant. It's easy to develop a fondness for the tall, regal carriage of this and other large *Cattleya* species, such as *C. guttata* var. *Leopoldii,* which I call Leopoldii to silence the botanical controversy, at least in my own mind. My specimen blooms most years before Christmas with many olive flowers spotted with brown dots. Its lip is a blush white, and it has a spade tongue of almost magenta hue. Although you should allow this orchid to dry out after flowering, maintain the humidity around the plant.

C. skinneri This is deservedly Costa Rica's national flower. In that country, I have seen specimens in colors ranging from orange through red to pure white. Although *C. skinneri* is one of the species protected by international treaties, it is commonly available from North American growers and nurseries that have started species swarms which live their entire lives in greenhouses. Mine is an iridescent lavender shade that lights up a room. I have grown it for a decade without dividing it by simply taking it out of the old pot and putting it in a new one, first shaking off the compost without disturbing the roots too much. When this orchid is repotted, there should be about two inches between the plant and the edge of the pot. The new pot will allow for a couple of years' growth. Repot after flowering. Keep humid and slightly dry until new growths show roots, then increase watering and apply a mild fertilizer. *C. skinneri* blooms around Easter for me.

C. forbesii A perfect windowsill orchid that grows less than a foot tall, with three or four tan-colored flowers up to four inches across and a pale pink, tubular lip which is deep yellow inside and marked with red veining. This plant is easily recognized by its pencil-like pseudobulbs. It blooms spring to summer.

***Laeliocattleya Culminant* 'La Tuilerie'** My favorite pink-flowered *Cattleya* hybrid comes from France and, when bloomed properly, has two or three six-inch flowers per stem. It's a true pink, not just a lavender color, and the contrasting lip and heavy scent make this a knockout. Don't give it more than 14 hours of light of any sort in the winter, or it won't bloom in the spring. It can be bloomed in a window if kept outdoors during the summer.

***Brassocattleya* Binosa** This is one of the best examples of the curious yet fortuitous possibilities of orchid hybridization. *Brassavola nodosa*, the most common roadside orchid south of the U.S. border, was crossed with *C. bicolor.* The offspring usually take the predominant shape of *B. nodosa* and have five thin, apple-green petals and a wide, flat lip spotted with pink. The flowers are charming, easy to grow in intermediate conditions and sport a variety of unusual colors.

Laelia purpurata *L. purpurata* looks like a cattleya and has added its influence to hybrids for a century. It is happiest in the greenhouse, where it can grow two to three feet tall. Its flowers have creamy white petals and a lip of purplish crimson. *L. purpurata* likes cool conditions, as do many orchids from Brazil.

Laelia autumnalis* or its variety *L. gouldiana These plants are even further removed from the conventional *Cattleya* tribe members. They are two of a number of interesting Mexican orchids with short, fat pseudobulbs and long, swordlike leaves. They fill a pot with clumps of pseudobulbs and throw out one spike from each new bulb, ending with big, star-shaped, rose-colored flowers bunched near the top. They bloom for me fall through winter.

***Epidendrum atropurpureum*, one of the largest members of the genus.**

Called the virgin orchid, Diacrium bicornutum is worthwhile, if challenging.

Epidendrum This is a varied and underrated genus among orchid growers. We all seem to have some, but they are never the stars of our collections, unless the plant is something unusual like *E. pseudepidendrum*. The family takes many shapes. The flowers, although often small, are plentiful and colorful. I have had much pleasure from growing *E. alatum*, with its squat bulbs and spikes of khaki flowers with purple spotting. Probably everyone's favorite is *E. atropurpureum*.

E. atropurpureum is always an eye-catcher when it blooms in late spring. Sepals and petals are a mix of green and mahogany. The huge lip ranges in color from white with crimson stripes to a perfect old rose. There are up to 10 attractively scented two-to-three-inch flowers on a short stem. Like most epidendrums, it appreciates intermediate conditions.

Rhyncholaelia digbyana I learned to love this plant as *Brassavola digbyana*, but taxonomists now tell us that this species and its only relative, *B. glauca*, must be moved from the *Brassavola* genus to a new one, *Rhyncholaelia*. The trouble is, many *Cattleya* hybrids were made with the species under the old name, and so-called Brassos are a distinct variety among cattleyas. So the old name remains for horticultural purposes. My *R. digbyana* refused to bloom for years, and it barely stayed alive from season to season. Finally, I removed it from the pot and mounted it on a piece of cork. The roots of this species abhor any moisture retention whatever, and I was constantly finding the roots rotted out in pots, no matter how coarse the potting material. When the flowers finally appeared after transfer to the cork, they came singly, but they're up to four inches across and an ice-green color with an unusual big, fringed lip. To "repot" the plant, I simply secure it, cork and all, to a larger piece of cork so that the plant can grow without interruption. It blooms in early spring.

Diacrium bicornutum The first time I saw this species in bloom, there were hundreds of them clinging to stone cliff faces overlooking the ocean in a remote part of the Caribbean island of Tobago. When I tried growing them at home, I found I couldn't duplicate the size of pseudobulbs the plants develop in the constant sunshine and humidity of their native home. I get much reduced blooming, but this species is still worth growing and deserves its name "virgin orchid." The flowers are white and vaguely star-shaped and have a very attractive presence and form. It blooms in summer while outdoors. This plant grows well under high-intensity lights.

DENDROBIUM

In a recent series of articles on dendrobiums, Scottish plantsman Richard Warren wrote of a trip to New Guinea: "As you climb from the swampy lowlands, home of the antelope dendrobiums, through the rainforest . . . you enter a moss forest. This is the orchidist's dream, so rich in plants and variety. Not only orchids drape from the trees; myriad ferns, gesneriads and begonias drip from the branches, and each branch and trunk is completely coated with moss, giving it a unique little climatic world of its own."

The name *Dendrobium* translates from the Latin to "living on trees," which just about describes this interesting genus with roughly 1,400 species. They're all epiphytic and grow in a bewildering number of habitats throughout Asia and as far south as Australia and New Zealand. They take so many shapes and forms that I leave it to the taxonomist to sort out what is a *Dendrobium* and what isn't. I simply enjoy cultivating them.

I grow everything from *Dendrobium senile*, with its tufted pseudobulbs and yellow flowers, to *D. phalaenopsis*, with spikes of butterfly-shaped flowers in white to magenta. A friend grows one of the antelope-horned hybrids on a tray in her bay window year-round. Hers flowers in a lovely coral color. *D. antennatum* and *D. phalaenopsis* are part of a group called evergreen dendrobiums that like con stant warm conditions. Other dendrobiums from various climates in their Asian range won't bloom without a dry rest period for up to several months. Some need a cold snap. Deciduous dendrobiums lose their leaves during the rest period. They are a little harder to master than the evergreens.

Evergreen Culture. Evergreen dendrobiums have pseudobulbs that are more spindle-shaped than the deciduous group. They are best planted in shallow terra-cotta pots, like azalea pots. The pseudobulbs, which can be four feet tall, tend to wave around in

Heat-loving Dendrobium phalaenopsis hybrids, **left,** *are easy to grow.* **Below,** *the multiple blooms of a Dendrobium aggregatum.*

DENDROBIUM (EVERGREEN) BASICS: A CHECKLIST

LIGHT: *1,500–2,500 footcandles*

TEMPERATURE: *60° to 80°F*

HUMIDITY: *50 to 70 percent*

FERTILIZER: *30-10-10 while actively growing*

WATER: *Moist at all times*

COMPOST: *Fir bark*

REST: *None*

the breeze, so a solid base is an advantage. Because evergreens grow continually and bloom when the latest bulb has matured, there are many flowerings throughout the year. I've grown several hybrids of this group and found them to be extremely rewarding, but they must never be exposed to cold temperatures. Keep them at 60 to 90 degrees F. Temperatures below 50 degrees can cause leaf drop.

The other popular member of the evergreen group, *D. phalaenopsis*, comes from Australia and New Guinea, and it, too, flowers profligately. I once grew a flaskful of *D. phalaenopsis* hybrid seedlings to maturity, and by the time I managed to get rid of the first batch of flowering plants, they had taken over about half of my little greenhouse. I was looking for that Holy Grail of orchid growers, the perfect prizewinning seedling. I never did find it, but I did grow a lot of *D. phalaenopsis* in a variety of magenta and purple shades.

Deciduous Culture. High light is in order for all dendrobiums, but especially deciduous ones, and many will take full outdoor light with relish once they are acclimated. Optimum light levels range from 2,000 to 4,000 footcandles. Deciduous dendrobiums like cooler weather. Some have survived down to 20 degrees F. Despite the vast number of species, most growers restrict themselves to a small cross section of the showier ones.

D. nobile hybrids like plenty of warmth and moisture in the summer,

For best blooming, Dendrobium pierardii needs cool temperatures.

then a cool rest in winter until flower buds appear along the canes. But don't water too soon, or instead of flowers, you'll get the dreaded *keiki*, tiny versions of the mother plant that appear from the nodes in the canes. Many *D. nobile* hybrids are prone to this unless watered at the proper time. *D. chrysanthum* and *D. wardianum*, two species, are also culturally in this group.

Members of yet another group of dendrobiums have deciduous leaves that last a couple of years. *D. aggregatum* is a good example of this group. It carries drooping masses of perky yellow flowers with a delightful scent and seems to grow best on rafts of cork, where its roots can dry out. I've seen these plants on village hut walls in northern Thailand, where they are grown on rafts of hardwood, and on trees in India, where they bake in the hot sun much of the summer. All members of the deciduous leaved group like intermediate to warm temperatures all year long, but they still demand that winter rest. Others in this group include *D. speciosum*, *D. findlayanum*, *D. pierardii*, *D. parishii* and *D. heterocarpum*. Some of these are good candidates for a bright, cool windowsill in the winter.

All dendrobiums enjoy a summer outing, with plenty of the good life to carry them over their ascetic winter fast. But many won't flower if their pleasant summer lives continue into winter. Leaving them outside until the temperature reaches 55 degrees F is often the only way to encourage them to flower.

Dendrobiums have fine root systems and seem to like underpotting in small pots so that their shoes get tight and their roots grow over the sides of the pot. I use medium fir bark and plenty of chunky charcoal to pot established dendrobiums. Use finer grades of both to start a plant with a smaller root system. Potting in a smaller pot also makes it less likely that dendrobiums will remain wet during their often extensive dry period.

Here are some I like to grow:

D. moschatum The long canes bloom in summer when they throw out one or two spikes of 7 to 10 flowers from near the top of the leafless older canes. The flowers, like slippers of old gold, bloom for only a couple of weeks and have an interesting spicy scent. Give plenty of water and fertilizer while the new growth is forming, then allow to dry out completely. Water only if the canes are shriveling alarmingly. Be strict.

D. kingianum This is a rugged little plant from Australia with small flowers that range from white to deep rose. It is able to survive almost any horticultural treatment and still flower occasionally, which it should do in winter. I grow mine on osmunda

Revival Techniques for Imported Orchids

I've had orchids delivered in everything from plastic bags to primitive rush baskets. With the concern for our dwindling fauna and flora these days, it's much rarer to receive jungle-collected plants. But when orchids do arrive desiccated, with roots that appear to be lifeless, I soak the entire plant in a mild solution of sugar and water for a day. This seems to work better than plain water. Then I put the orchids in an enclosed propagator shaded from direct sunlight. The plants rest on a bed of moistened sphagnum moss. Freshly collected green moss is best if it is free of bugs. I find mine in moist woods, but soaked New Zealand sphagnum is good. With the propagator open slightly, air gets to the plants, but high humidity is encouraged. Roots can revive and grow quickly in this atmosphere. Once roots have appeared, I pot up the plant.

crammed into a little wallet fashioned from chicken wire. It hangs on a sunny wall in my greenhouse, but before I had a greenhouse, I grew it in a clay pot tightly packed with osmunda or fine fir bark. Grow intermediate to cold.

D. densiflorum This orchid looks spectacular in bloom, with lush hanging scapes of orange-centered, butter-yellow flowers that often completely encircle the plant. They have a pleasing crystalline texture that is a characteristic of many dendrobiums. *D. densiflorum* blooms in the spring after a dry winter.

D. pierardii To me, this species carries the classic charm gene of dendrobiums. Imagine a plant growing, canes hanging from the branch of a tree, bare of leaves in the Indian sun, covered along its length with pairs of pale pink flowers with yellow lips, striped in purple. They love plenty of sun and then a good drying out. New growths appear about the same time as the scented flowers. It blooms for me in late winter to spring.

D. spectabile This is one of the showier members of the vast family of New Guinea dendrobiums. With their curious yet attractive shapes, orchids from this group are all the rage these days among *Dendrobium* fanciers. All species in this family are worth growing, although some may appreciate much more radical culture than *D. spectabile*. Water steadily. Flowers appear in the spring.

Dendrobium spectabile is famous for its twisted and colorful flowers.

Cymbidium Velvet Fire is one of the thousands of cool-temperature-loving cymbidiums cultivated by hobbyists.

Cymbidium

If a grower has the right conditions, cymbidiums can be simple to cultivate. I envy orchidists on the West Coast and in parts of Australia and New Zealand, who have the climate cymbidiums like: no higher than 95 degrees F in summer and no lower than 35 degrees in winter. These plants need steady watering year-round and a breezy atmosphere, with shade from full sun and protection from too much heat in the hottest months.

Cymbidiums are certainly spectacular: big terrestrial orchids with spikes of three-inch flowers in bold, rich colors from white through green, yellow, orange, red and purple, in many shades and shapes. When the pseudobulb has matured in the autumn, I like to keep the plant outside, but away from the autumn rains, so that the cold night air will initiate the flower spikes.

There are about 60 *Cymbidium* species that come from mountain regions as well as warmer areas. Horticulturally, cymbidiums are divided into a couple of groups.

The large flowers of the commercial varieties live in tubs too big to move without a handcart and are the most popular cut flowers in the world, because they last a long time and come in huge sprays. These hybrids, like *Cymbidium Alexanderi* 'Westonbirt,' need the big, cool living quarters that a greenhouse can provide. Try one if you have a large, cool sunroom.

Easier to handle and not so strict in their demands are the miniature

CYMBIDIUM BASICS: A CHECKLIST

Light: *2,000–4,000 footcandles*

Temperature: *45° to 90°F*

Humidity: *40 to 60 percent*

Fertilizer: *Half-strength 20-20-20 until flowering, then no feeding until new growths*

Water: *Consistent moisture*

Compost: *Bark or terrestrial mix with forest compost*

Rest: *None*

cymbidiums. These were produced by crossing back regular large *Cymbidium* hybrids with true miniature cymbidiums from warmer climates, like *C. pumilum*, *C. devonianum*, *C. ensifolium*, *C. tigrinum*, *C. dayanum* and *C. elegans*. The miniaturization has met with various degrees of success, depending on who has done the crossing. There are, in fact, "miniatures" that rival the regular standard cymbidiums in size. Cymbidiums with plenty of *C. pumilum* or *C. devonianum* in their backgrounds are among the smallest, most floriferous plants, although the *C. devonianum* flower spike tends to hang down the side of the plant, rather than stand straight up. Cymbidiums of any sort tend not to bloom until they are ready for bigger pots; six inches is the smallest pot size I've seen on a flowering plant.

Growers have been fiddling with *Cymbidium* potting mixes for years, trying to come up with something that will last. The cheapest solution for me has been a mix of medium and fine fir bark. Some growers add bone meal or slow-release fertilizer pellets so that the plant is fed automatically when it is watered. Cymbidiums grow with gay abandon if kept outside in the summer and watered with a hose.

The miniatures can be grown with cattleyas. Crosses are too numerous to name, although the Peter Pan breeding line is a famous one. Miniatures with *C. ensifolium* often inherit a delightful scent and a late-summer flowering period. Much interesting work is currently being done by Australian and New Zealand growers to produce miniature cymbidiums with strong, clear colors.

Repotting cymbidiums when you finally have to can be a problem, because these plants tend to fill their pots with roots as thick as earthworms. A mature cymbidium in a 14-inch pot may literally have to have an ax taken to it. Split the plant so that each new division has at least a newly forming pseudobulb along with a few back bulbs, preferably still with leaves.

It is very important to the overall health of cymbidiums to keep the temperature at around 50 to 55 degrees F at night during autumn, winter and spring and never over 85 degrees at any time of the year. These temperatures are ideals and are virtually impossible to attain in some parts of the world, even in shade. Yet many growers successfully cultivate cymbidiums.

After watching a few prize cymbidiums deteriorate over the years, I have come to the conclusion that heat prostration finally weakens the plants, so they succumb in the end, especially if hit by disease or an attack of bugs. Some orchidists who feel they simply must have cymbidiums have resorted to air conditioning to grow their favorite plants. I must confess, I just buy a new one now and then.

Wherever cymbidiums are grown, they like plenty of ventilation and humidity, with some shade in summer and lots of sunshine in winter. This allows the pseudobulbs to mature and plump up, so when the cool weather comes again, they readily throw spikes. Sometimes, there is confusion about what is a flower spike and what is a new growth. Because they look very much alike at an early stage, a new grower may buy what appears to be a mature plant ready

***Cymbidium tigrinum*, top, *likes warmth*. Above, *Cymbidium Nathaniel*.**

A hybrid form of Phalaenopsis amabilis shows the highly desirable rounded contours sought by breeders.

to flower, only to find it isn't.

The flower spike emerges from the base of the most newly mature bulb shortly after the initiation of dry, cool conditions for the plant. Since a new growth looks similar in the early stages, examine the plant for a bulge in the top of the growth. If it has one, it's probably a flower spike. If it's thicker at the base, with a more pointed top, it's just a new lead. I plunge a thin bamboo stake into the pot when the spike is six to eight inches high and secure the spike to the stake at intervals with green garbage-bag ties. The arrangement looks quite inconspicuous, since the bamboo is also green.

C. devonianum My plant came from Nepal and flowers for me in early spring, producing pendent, arching spikes of tawny green flowers with a purple, triangular lip. *C. devonianum* is easy to grow in intermediate temperatures without a cooling period.

C. eburneum Although one of the building blocks of *Cymbidium* hybridization, *C. eburneum* is not a willing grower. When flowers do appear, they are white to ivory with a yellow band in the lip. I issue warnings like this because some exporters sell plants collected in the wild that seem to be particularly hard to establish.

PHALAENOPSIS

There are about 50 species of this excellent genus based on the beautiful white *Phalaenopsis amabilis*, an orchid first described in 1753 by the the father of modern botany, Carolus Linnaeus. They come mostly from dense, wet forests in an area extending from India through Southeast Asia, the Philippines and into northern Australia. There, they grow as epiphytes, with daily temperatures around 95 degrees F and night temperatures 20 degrees cooler. Because of this, it's important never to allow Phals to go below 60 degrees in cultivation. They tend to regress very quickly if exposed to cold temperatures.

Most growers today cultivate hybrids whose genetic path lines have been blurred sufficiently so that a more general culture can be applied successfully. *Phalaenopsis* species, for instance, have more demanding cultural needs than *Phalaenopsis* hybrids. This is especially true in such species as *P. violacea* and *P. gigantea*. On the

PHALAENOPSIS BASICS: A CHECKLIST

LIGHT: ***Bright, light shadow***
TEMPERATURE: ***65° to 85°F***
HUMIDITY: ***40 to 70 percent***
FERTILIZER: ***Balanced, quarter-strength weekly***
WATER: ***Do not allow to dry out***
COMPOST: ***Medium fir bark***
REST: ***None***

Left: ***One of the many color forms of Phalaenopsis lueddemanniana.*** ***Phalaenopsis schilleriana,*** **below,** ***carries hundreds of delicate pink blossoms.*** **Bottom:** ***Representative shapes and colors of Phalaenopsis flowers.***

other hand, I can't think of any species easier to grow than *P. lueddemanniana*, with its 30 color forms.

Even though phalaenopsises grow quickly from seed to flowering stage, their general growth pattern is slow. As monopodial orchids, they put out only a couple of leaves a year. And because they are monopodial, mericloning is out. But they do reproduce from offshoots, particularly if the plant is stressed. New plants, complete with roots, sometimes appear on the spike where the flower nodes are or around the base of the old plant. There are a number of ointments on the market that encourage the formation of new plants through hormone action. Until quite recently, this has been the only way to get exact copies of desirable Phals.

High humidity is important for Phals. They have no water-storage organs and so must have a constantly moist environment. Seventy percent humidity is not too much, and it can be attained by placing the plants on trays of stones sitting in water. Air is also important and should be kept moving with a fan. It's perhaps easier to keep up humidity in Phals because they like a shaded atmosphere year-round.

I like to spray my plants during the day to maintain the humidity, but I'm careful not to let water settle in the crown of the leaves. Some growers tip their plants slightly in the pots to prevent water from causing crown rot, which is just about the quickest way to kill a phalaenopsis. And watch those roots! Phalaenopsis roots are thicker than many and are designed both to anchor the plant and to manufacture some of its nutrient needs. Try not to lose too many roots, because they develop slowly and there are not that many to begin with.

***Cypripedium calceolus*, a North American member of the vast *Paphiopedilum* clan.**

Phals are now available in so many colors that I advise newcomers to wait until the plants are in flower before buying. Do you like stripes, red lips, big whites, yellows, dots, oranges or deep, deep reds? These are all recent trends in *Phalaenopsis* breeding, and their success is best judged by the beholder. Also, the visual difference between a very expensive Phal and one that costs around $20 can be tiny. My advice to the beginning Phalophile is to start cheap and cheerful.

P. schilleriana The ideal species, *P. schilleriana* can carry a hundred light pink flowers on branched stems. Its leaves, mottled greyish white and purple underneath, are pretty, even without the flowers. Small and compact, the plant is used to enhance branching in hybrids. It flowers in spring.

P. stuartiana This looks like a white-flowered cousin of *P. schilleriana*. It, too, has branching stems and is used to increase branching in hybrids. Such hybrids often have the characteristic blush of purple spots around the base of the petals.

P. lueddemanniana This small plant has many color forms, including *P. hieroglyphica* and *P. lueddemanniana* var. *ochracea*, and is often confused with *P. mariae*. My plant throws new flower spikes when the old ones have matured and has been flowering continuously since I bought it two years ago. This is a common characteristic of the less showy Phal species.

Doritis pulcherrima A relative of the phalaenopsis, this orchid was introduced to Phal hybrids to intensify the red/purple colors. Phals with this combination are called *Doritaenopsis*.

Paphiopedilum fairieanum*, left: *A reward of thousands of dollars was once offered for the rediscovery of this now common species.* Below, *Paphiopedilum armeniacum.

PAPHIOPEDILUM

When I first started in orchids, paphiopedilums were called cypripediums, or Cyps, among knowledgeable growers. That made perfect sense, since cypripediums of northern temperate regions are members of the *Paphiopedilum* family and essentially look the same. Lady's-slipper orchids are a common example. Culturally, though, they have different needs.

Botanists have divided paphiopedilums into four groups, and horticulturists have gone along.

Members of the *Cypripedium* family need a cool period in winter before flowering is initiated in early spring. They also require specific bog conditions to bloom successfully and so are unsuitable for most growers. They transplant extremely poorly unless a proper bed is prepared.

Species of *Phragmipedium* often have dazzlingly twisted petals that are more than a foot and a half long and may drape on the ground, where ants are said to follow them as trails to pollinate the flowers. Phragmipediums, which come from South America, seem to like constantly wet conditions.

The genus *Selenipedium* is essentially a horticultural curiosity, with its eight-foot-tall flowering stems topped with clusters of drooping pouched flowers. It comes from grassy country, where height is a prerequisite in order to compete for pollinators. It, too, is South American.

Finally, there is *Paphiopedilum*, from Asia. There are 60 species that grow from the cool Indian Himalayas to small, hot, rock-covered archipelagoes in the South China Sea. They come in a variety of pouched configurations and colors, and the species are as much fun to grow as are the complex hybrids that have been painstakingly created over the past century. The discovery of a new *Paphiopedilum* species always arouses interest in this sometimes easy-to-grow genus. The latest fad is the

Chinese Paphs, like *Paphiopedilum armeniacum*, with enormous pouches in butter-yellow colors and heavenly pinks and tans. Export of these plants was cut off several years ago, so until some enterprising orchidist manages to raise greenhouse-grown populations, individual seedlings are precious.

That's one of the problems with this genus. Paphs are often mean with their seed. Some complex hybrids produce only a dusting of seed and a few plants that grow to maturity. This translates into big prices for some plants. For me, though, there's always been plenty of excitement just trying to keep up with the spectacular variety of the color khaki in *Paphiopedilum* species.

An easy-to-grow Paphiopedilum venustum.

Imagine a forest floor, and you will know how paphiopedilums like to live. They enjoy subdued light, which is one reason why they are so popular in temperate climates. Combine this with gentle breezes and plenty of moisture at the roots, and you pretty much have the ideal climate for any paphiopedilum. Many paphiopedilums make perfect windowsill-mates for your phalaenopsises, because they both enjoy similar light conditions as well as temperatures.

I grow mine wetter in the summer under shading in my greenhouse. My paphiopedilums like a potting mixture of bark and medium perlite, to which I sometimes add charcoal and strands of sphagnum moss. They grow better when surrounded by other Paphs or even other kinds of plants. This propinquity increases the humidity around the plants and makes them perkier.

I've picked up most of my Paphs from the members' sales table at my orchid society. People are always discarding things which they don't like or which aren't in fashion. So my own collection has grown eccentrically, depending on what was available. There are some wonderful hybrids, but many are out of my price range, and their sometimes steroidal shapes are not to my liking. For a Paph fanatic, of course, no price is too much.

I've found that the easiest Paphs to grow are species and primary hybrids, which often have enhanced strength from that initial crossing. The trick to Paphs is a continuous but not cloying moisture around the roots. Since they like a porous and fluffy compost, Paphs should be repotted every couple of years. Shake out the old compost, and dip the plant in a bucket of water to get rid of the loosely clinging stuff. I'm always surprised at how decomposed it can become in just a year, so I try not to neglect repotting.

Culturally, paphiopedilums are divided into two broad groups: green leaves, which need cool temperatures, and mottled leaves, which need warm temperatures. (One exception to this rule is *P. venustum*, a mottled-leaf plant that I grow and bloom around Christmastime under cool conditions.) Ideally, the green leaves would go into the cool house with the cymbidiums, and the mottled leaves would bask in the warm breezes of the phalaenopsis house. Actually, I grow mine all mixed together from windowsill to greenhouse to deck, depending on where the conditions are right.

The right conditions mean low light: up to 1,200 footcandles. I suspend black greenhouse shading on the outside of my growing windows to reduce the amount of heat and light that reaches the Paphs. In the greenhouse, that means draping extra shading over the area where most of the plants are kept. A healthy Paph can grow very large, especially when it likes its environment. Keeping the humidity high is a key to good Paph growing. Many seem to grow out of the compost after they have been in a pot for a while. This potting problem can affect the new root growth. I usually bury the plant deep and top up once with a sprinkling of compost, so the bottom leaves are always slightly below the top of the compost. Roots can then proceed normally, as they do in nature, slightly below the surface of the compost. When I divide Paphs, I leave at least two growths per pot: the new one, which has no roots yet, and the one it's attached to, which does have roots

Commonly called the "hairy one," Paphiopedilum hirsutissimum is a good intermediate-temperature orchid.

and nourishes the plant until the new growth is established.

Paphs need a light feeding schedule. As with most orchids, fertilizers with more nitrogen are given during the warmest months. As the year's growth matures, fertilizer with a high phosphorus content, or middle number, is applied to enhance flower growth. Most Paphs are good candidates for outdoor culture in the summer, particularly in temperate climates, where the nip in the air at the end of the growing season often sparks flowering.

P. venustum I grow this for its marvelous marbled foliage of gray, green and dark purple. It flowers around Christmas for me, with single blossoms in shades of tan, green, pink and purple, with spots and hairs. It has serenely complicated flowers that last a month or more. I cultivate *P. venustum* at temperatures between 60 and 80 degrees F, but extremes are flexible. This orchid has grown in the 40-degree range for me, and I've had it in the greenhouse for a day or so with temperatures well over 100 degrees.

P. hirsutissimum This green-leaf

PAPHIOPEDILUM BASICS: A CHECKLIST

LIGHT: *600-2,000 footcandles; bright shade*

TEMPERATURE: *Cool Paphs: 50° to 75°F. Warm Paphs: 60° to 80°F*

HUMIDITY: *40 to 60 percent*

FERTILIZER: *30-10-10 in bark; 20-20-20 in terrestrial mix*

WATER: *Continuous moisture*

COMPOST: *Bark or fluffy terrestrial mix*

REST: *None*

Phragmipedium Grande, **left.**

Paph species is colored in hairy shades of purple and green. Hence the name, meaning "hairy one." It grows at temperatures between 60 and 80 degrees F and flowers in late winter after a slight drying out.

P. primulinum This pretty, yellow, continuous-flowering Paph from Sumatra was only described in 1973. The flowers are small, but they seem to grow on and on. Its cousin, *P. glaucophyllum*, has the same physical proportions, but the colors are different, with combinations of green, rose, white and speckled reds. Grow between 60 and 80 degrees F or a little warmer, with no rest.

P. insigne A Himalayan species that is very easy to grow at slightly cooler temperatures than the Paphs mentioned above. The single flowers have a tan pouch, yellow-green spotted dorsal sepal and petals of khaki.

P. purpuratum A native of Hong Kong, this orchid has a distinctly wine-purple pouch and petals, a jaunty striped dorsal sepal and pretty marbled foliage. This is an easy grower for windowsill or greenhouse. Temperature: 50 to 75 degrees F for green; 60 to 80 degrees for mottled.

PHRAGMIPEDIUM

As growers unlock their secrets, more of these beautiful South American cousins of the Asian paphiopedilums are being cultivated by hobbyists every year.

I flower *Phragmipedium Sedenii*, an old primary hybrid. It has more erect pink flowers than most Phrags and is a loyal bloomer for me in late spring, with plenty of pouched flowers coming in succession over a month or so. Phrags did not grow well for me until I increased my watering so that the roots not only were constantly wet but had fresh water reapplied at regular intervals. This fits in with the natural life style of Phrags, many of which grow by the sides of streams.

Phrags also like a little more sunshine than paphiopedilums. A south window with up to 2,000 footcandles is good. Temperatures shouldn't go too much below 58 degrees F at night or 85 degrees during the day.

A genus in their own right, oncidiums form part of a large orchid "family" whose members have been genetically crossed since the last century. **Left,** *Oncidium ampliatum, the so-called tortoise-shell orchid.*

ONCIDIUM

Although *Oncidium* is a separate genus, I think of these orchids as part of a great family of allied plants—some look similar; some look radically different—that make good mates and produce pleasing offspring when crossed with each other. In its purest form, this family comprises *Oncidium,* of course, but also *Odontoglossum, Miltonia, Brassia, Aspasia, Cochlioda* and several other more obscure genera. Since the last century, breeders have been combining the various species to produce new genera, such as *Vuylstekeara, Sanderara* and *Beallara.*

These human-made genera tend to be difficult to grow, because they need conditions that combine the attributes of all the parents. That's not to say that among the complex hybrids, I haven't found vuylstekearas, such as *Vuylstekeara* 'Cambria Plush' FCC/AM/AOS, that are easier to grow than many of their kin, requiring only intermediate conditions. But by and large, it's best to start with a few species or primary hybrids. Primary hybrids, which are crosses between two species, are usually the most vigorous hybrids. Broadly speaking, their culture can be divided into a few general categories.

Oncidium henekenii, **above,** *mimics a bee to attract pollinators. Oncidium Magic Touch (O. Passionata Red x O. henekenii),* **right,** *shows traits of its henekenii parent.*

For instance, a hybrid containing *Oncidium* would like a drier, sunnier location and would possess smaller

Odontoglossum bictoniense, the first of the genus to be introduced to Europe.

flowers, but more of them, than a hybrid crossed with *Odontoglossum*, which needs shadier, cooler and moister conditions. A hybrid dominated by *Miltonia* would appreciate moist, intermediate to warm conditions. Its flowers would be more star-shaped, probably with large lips.

With more than 750 species, oncidiums grow anywhere from sea level to an elevation of 13,000 feet, so their culture can vary a good deal, but there are some general rules: These plants like plenty of light and definite dry periods between good soakings at the roots, but they don't like it if their roots are cramped or kept constantly moist. When plants are growing leaves and bulbs, I feed while watering, but when bulbs are fat and round, I water sparsely. The humidity should be kept to at least 60 percent. All oncidiums seem to enjoy vigorous breezes and, when receiving them, can take more moisture and consequently grow faster. The only limiting factor, then, is the amount of light.

I grow oncidiums in clay pots with coarse compost, which seems to keep the roots drier, or on cork slabs. Cork requires daily spraying if the roots are to get enough moisture. Cork and rafts are a great way to grow plants, but they need automatic spraying, which usually means a greenhouse.

O. splendidum I've grown mine for more than a dozen years, and it blooms faithfully in early spring. This is one of the "mule ear" oncidiums, with short bulbs and angular, rigid leaves that seem to belong to a desert plant. The sepals and petals are insignificant compared with the lip, which is a rich buttery yellow. It likes to go out in summer and produces really big leaves and bulbs. Eventually, it rewards me with branched spikes and dozens of flowers.

O. ampliatum This plant's branched flower stems can grow three feet tall. The so-called dancing dolls are yellow spotted with red, and the round lip is cream-colored on the underside. My plant grows on cork bark and is easy to identify because the pseudobulbs look like wrinkled turtle shells. This is one of those species that blooms easily but hates to grow in a pot.

O. flexuosum This one likes to ramble, but its panicles of many bright yellow flowers make up for any awkwardness. *O. flexuosum* can be grown on a hardwood log or wound around an osmunda ball in a large clay pot. Don't fence it in, and it will flourish.

ODONTOGLOSSUM

Found in the mountain regions in Central and South America, odontoglossums need cool conditions, with temperatures never above 80 degrees

F, if it can be helped. They make ideal companion plants for cymbidiums. Because they come from areas that are bathed in cool mists every day, odontoglossums are best—but not necessarily—grown in greenhouses, where they can receive plenty of moisture and brisk breezes, conditions as close as possible to those in their native homes.

I have tried a number of odontoglossums over the years and have found the following easy to grow even without the benefit of a greenhouse:

O. bictoniense The hardiness of this Central American orchid is demonstrated by the fact that it was the first *Odontoglossum* species to survive the long sea voyage from Central America to England. It has yellow-green sepals and petals and a white to rose lip.

O. grande Flowers can be five to nine inches across, which makes this Mexico/Guatemala native a very popular odontoglossum around the world. Needs less cool temperatures than most in this genus. I've seen good specimens bloomed under lights, with yellow-and-brown barred flowers.

O. pulchellum I've grown these Central American natives for years, despite the unimpressive, small white flowers shaped like bird heads. I like the interesting reedy foliage and the wonderful perfume the little flowers emit. In that way, *O. pulchellum* is somewhat like the lily of the valley orchids.

A word of advice: Unless you have cool, moist, breezy conditions in your home or grow in a greenhouse, stay away from the Andean odontoglossums—*O. crispum* and its hybrids—even though they are by far the most beautiful. First, try your hand at the Mexican and Central American odontoglossums, like the three discussed above, which can be grown more easily in a mixed collection.

MILTONIA

Viscount Milton, a great gardener of his day, would have gone totally unremembered were it not for the fateful decision to name this very pretty genus after him in 1837. The so-called pansy orchids have broad, flat flowers in bright colors, with face masks that make them resemble characters out of *Alice's Adventures in Wonderland.* The thin, sword-shaped foliage complements the look of branched flowers on a well-grown plant.

Horticulturists divide the genus into two groups: the Andean miltonias, with rounded flowers bearing colored masks and waterfall patterns of dots; and the Brazilian miltonias, with more star-shaped flowers. The

Miltoniopsis Bert Field 'Crimson Glow,' with its typical Andean pansy shape.

two groups are cultivated in different ways.

The mountain species are represented by small plants with big flowers in red, white and yellow tones, with masks of color in the center. These plants like cool, moist conditions and a narrow range of temperatures—no warmer than 60 degrees F at night and 80 degrees during the day. Such temperatures are difficult to maintain in most greenhouses during the summer. A few orchidists, however, have had great success with these miltonias and their hybrids under lights in cool basements, where many prizewinning miltonias are grown. Some species are pleasantly scented. Awarded mericlones of the best of these crosses are available at several outlets. Try *Miltonia Lycaena* 'Stamperland' FCC/RHS and any new hybrids that catch your eye.

The Brazilian group are miltonias from the lowlands of Central and South America. Although easily grown in a mixed collection at higher temperatures, they have more star-shaped flowers and flowers with dots and bars on them, which makes them less refined in the eyes of some orchid judges. Many of the Brazilians also bear their flowers at the end of a long spike, so their hybrids have a bunched look that is not in fashion these days. I've grown *M. flavescens*, which has long, dull yellow flowers that don't look too bad against the narrow foliage, and *M. Bluntii*, an old spotted primary hybrid in shades of brown, purple and cream. *M. Bluntii* blooms faithfully for me in early summer, wired to a cedar shingle on which it spreads its decorative foliage quite nicely. I like it because it is scented and easy to bloom and can tolerate my sometimes sporadic watering schedule. Many of the other species are more decorative than this, ranging from cream colors through purples, pinks and chestnut brown, with many pleasing shades and scents.

A heat-loving Miltonia clowesii.

While they do not like strong light, miltonias grow slightly brighter than paphiopedilums. They do very well under lights, although usually a special microclimate must be found to cultivate them happily in a greenhouse, where they like to be near misters. Miltonias are also finicky about where they park their roots, so any breakdown of the compost puts their wiry roots in danger. I have had success repotting annually in a mixture of fine grades of fir bark, perlite, charcoal and tree fern. These plants prefer small plastic pots so that the roots can fill the pot quickly.

Miltonias can be tricky, but as I've slowly unraveled their secrets, they have become more and more rewarding to grow. Since the blooms have such a variety of masks, I recommend buying plants in flower so that you see what you're getting. When grown well, miltonias make excellent specimen plants and can last for years, provided they are repotted regularly at the beginning of the growing season, which for me is spring.

Brassia

Who cannot help being fascinated by brassias, the spider orchids. Flowers can be 20 inches from the top of the narrow dorsal sepals to the equally narrow hanging petals. With their spotted gold, brown, green and cream flowers, they are irresistible curiosities. Most of my *Brassia* species and crosses have bloomed in summer, when they put on a spectacular show. The spidery form is reduced, somewhat, in intergeneric hybrids, but brassias generally turn anything they are bred with into a starry shape. Perhaps the prettiest hybrids occur between *Brassia* and *Odontoglossum.*

Brassia verrucosa, often called the spider orchid.

Brassias like to grow warm to intermediate, with plenty of moisture. A spike can have up to 20 spidery flowers.

B. gireoudiana These have the biggest flowers in the group. Native to Central America, they are an overall yellow-green color, with a creamy lip.

Male and female flowers of Catasetum fimbriatum are strikingly different.

CATASETUM

This is an orchid with more cousins than a mountain clan. *Catasetum* is the dominant genus in a tribe that comprises *Catasetum*, *Cycnoches*, *Mormodes*, *Gongora*, *Coryanthes* and *Stanhopea*. The flowers in these groups are curiously shaped, and many members, particularly among the catasetums, jettison their pollen at bees that alight to sip their nectar. This trait is endlessly fascinating for the amateur orchidist and, apparently, for the bees as well, because they keep coming back for more. It's actually difficult to keep the flowers alive for long, because sometimes merely jarring them can cause the pollinia to pop. Once the orchid's pollinia is spent, the flower changes color and begins to die.

Catasetums also have male and female flowers, often on the same plant, that look quite different from each other. Early botanists were confused by this and so renamed many catasetums that were already known to cultivation. It has since been discovered that a catasetum's sex depends to a large extent on both the amount and the intensity of sunlight it receives.

Catasetums and cycnoches, the swan orchids, have tall, fat pseudobulbs that lose their leaves after flowering and are very prone to rotting if water is applied too soon at the end of the resting period. Throughout much of the winter, my plants look like nothing more than a few pseudobulbs with a papery coating sticking out of a clay pot. Then, in early spring, a flush of green appears at the base of one or more of the pseudobulbs. This is *not* a signal to begin watering. Soon enough, thick, green-tipped white roots appear from the base of the green growth. After the roots have entered the dry compost, the plants can be watered by dipping, but don't let the base of the old pseudobulb get wet, or it will probably rot.

When the roots are growing well, throw watering caution to the wind. Daily soakings are not too much, especially when the plants are outside. I dip my plants in a solution of one-quarter cup fish emulsion in a three-gallon pail of water. The reason for this feeding frenzy is that the new shoots grow dramatically in the hot summer sun, especially when water and fertilizer are given in sufficient quantities to keep up with the increased sunlight outside.

Cut back on watering when the pseudobulbs have matured; this is easy to determine in any orchid because all the leaves will have unfolded that are going to unfold. The cooler, dry period is followed by the initiation of a spike, or several, from the base of the new pseudobulb. Some members of the *Catasetum* tribe throw spikes from higher up on the pseudobulb as well. All plants of this genus have interesting, curious blooms up to five inches across, in rich primary colors. Some of the hybrids are spectacular,

Vanda sanderiana var. alba is the species that established the genus and is now used extensively in hybridization.

with blood-red flowers or dainty chains of feathered pink blooms or teacup-sized, flat, icy green blossoms. Many also have hauntingly beautiful scents, for which they are valued far more than some of the better-known orchids of South and Central America.

C. pileatum Selected clones of this Venezuelan species are available in colors ranging from pure white through icy green to butter-yellow. With their classic flat shape, they are among the most beautiful of orchids.

C. macrocarpum Mine was collected off a fencepost in Costa Rica many years ago. These plants seem to pop up all over South and Central America and are among the easiest species to grow. They have different male/female flowers and look very odd when both are in bloom on the same plant.

Cycnoches chlorochilon All members of this group have the unusual trait among orchids of holding their flowers upside down. They are said to look like elegant birds, hence the popular name swan orchid. Flowers, in shades of green and yellow, are a pretty contrast to the light green leaves.

Vanda

Orchid growers speak of vandas, of course, but what they often mean these days is a plant with some *Vanda* in it.

So many new, brighter colors have been introduced by cousins like *Ascocentrum*, *Phalaenopsis*, *Renanthera*, *Aerides* and *Arachnis* that hardly any-

Vanda species and hybrids such as V. Bartle Frere x V. Manila revel in light.

one cultivates the old, big, straight vandas, unless they have plants that just won't die or they like *Vanda* species, which have a colorful charm of their own.

Most members of this group revel in light, with some able to take up to 8,000 footcandles. A few of the smaller *Vanda*-alliance members can be grown under lights.

Orchidists fortunate enough to live in Florida or Hawaii can even cultivate them outdoors, but most growers keep them in a sunroom or a greenhouse, where there is plenty of room to water them. Vandas like a total soaking, and some of the older hybrids are huge, standing taller than a man.

The smaller vandas grow best for me in hardwood baskets filled with wine corks pressed around the plants to hold them upright.

Vandas have to be misted every day and should never go below 60 degrees F, unless they carry plenty of genes from the blue Himalayan species *Vanda coerulea*, which likes it nippy at night. Keeping the temperature at 70 degrees is even better for most *Vanda* hybrids and results in lusher growth and more blooms.

Repotting vandas should be avoided if at all possible. Their roots resent it so much that it may take years for the plant to recover, if it ever resumes growing properly. That's why they grow so successfully in hardwood baskets, to which they can attach their thick roots, as in nature. Repotting is simply a matter of dropping the plant, basket and all, into a larger basket.

Unless they are cultivated in a hot climate, these monopodials will grow slowly. Wherever they are grown, they benefit from being outdoors as long as temperatures permit. There, they can be sprayed daily and fed a richer diet than most orchids, by either dipping them in a fertilizer solution or spraying the solution on the roots and leaves.

Stanhopea

Why would I recommend a plant that blooms for only seven days a year at most and takes up a lot of space while it gets ready to do that trick? Anyone who has seen the *Stanhopea* flower wouldn't ask. I limit myself to just a couple of plants: *Stanhopea wardii*, from Costa Rica, and *S. tigrina*.

Certain bees in the jungles have reportedly been attracted by the scent of stanhopeas from more than half a mile away, and I believe it. I can't stay out of the greenhouse when my stanhopeas are in bloom. Their heavy aroma permeates everything, even when the fans are on.

My specimen of *S. wardii* came from a few bulbs pulled off a huge clump that was growing on a tree in Costa Rica. It has since developed into its own large clump. Another curious fact about stanhopeas is that they have to be grown either in baskets or in pots with no bottoms. I use both methods. The reason is that flower spikes grow downward in this species, usually straight through the compost. Stories abound of gardeners cultivating stanhopeas for years and wondering why they wouldn't flower, until they repot and find the mummified remains of flower spikes that had tried to grow through the bottom of the pot but couldn't.

I keep mine in osmunda in an old hanging plastic pot that used to house

Madagascar native: Angraecum sesquipedale x A. eburneum

a fuchsia. I cut the bottom out of the pot and potted the plant loosely with osmunda. My other stanhopea grows in a big basket I made from chicken wire lined with a black plastic garbage bag in which I poked drainage holes. The potting medium is dry oak leaves and forest humus, which is one of my longest-lasting potting discoveries. I can tell when a flower is coming by the bulge that appears in the plastic. I carefully cut a slit, and the flower begins to grow through. The plastic is necessary, I've found; otherwise, the compost dries out too quickly.

I keep my plants uniformly moist all year, with perhaps a slight drying out when the bulb has formed. Then I wait impatiently as the flower spike develops and the four or five buds slowly fill up. When stanhopeas finally do flower, it is worth the wait.

Other Orchids I Like

Ansellia nilotica All the so-called species of this African orchid look about the same, except for the intensity of their colors, which are basically starry yellow flowers with brown spots. The blooms are about two inches across and have a nice scent. They grow in branched spikes from a two-foot-tall, spindle-shaped pseudobulb. Mine flower in a gorgeous upheld cascade in late spring, and I would miss this plant sorely if I didn't have it in my collection.

Trichopilia suavis The flowers of this genus are almost as large as the pseudobulb and leaf together. They are white and have a ruffled lip speckled with pink. *T. tortilis* has twisted, ribbonlike sepals and petals of brownish green, which contrast with the white lip. Some plants throw out a couple of flowers from each bulb. All are fragrant and prefer to be grown wet in a clay pot. They bloom in winter.

Above: ***An easy-to-grow Ansellia nilotica.*** **Right:** ***Hairs on Bulbophyllum barbigerum lure pollinators.***

Angraecum sesquipedale Extremely waxy white flowers can be up to eight inches across on this elegant monopodial. A distinguishing feature is a long, white spur that ends the flower. Charles Darwin is said to have predicted the evolution of a moth with a tongue long enough to reach the bottom of the nectary. The story goes that years after his death, such a moth was discovered. My *A. sesquipedale* blooms around Christmas, and the flower has been called the Star of Bethlehem.

Bulbophyllum Since there are some 2,000 species, I won't name a favorite. There are many interesting flower forms and shapes, with hinged lips, Medusa-like petals and forms that look like rosettes. Most prefer warm, moist conditions, with good drainage. Some orchidists grow only these interesting Asian species.

Calanthe vestita This terrestrial has oddly shaped angular bulbs. It makes a good windowsill specimen and likes plenty of water in a humusy compost while the new bulbs are forming. At the end of summer, water is withheld entirely until the leaves fall off. After a couple of months, a flower spike and new growths will appear. Watering is then resumed. The flowers come in white to red colors.

Lycaste aromatica The great *Lycaste* tribe deserves a book of its own and has had at least one. Lycastes grow from Mexico to Central America and look elegant with their shiny bulbs topped with broad leaves. Plenty of water during the warm season is followed by cooler, drier conditions when lycastes bloom. They often lose all their leaves in winter, and with up to 10 flowers per bulb, the plant looks like a forest of flowers.

Masdevallia coccinea This plant likes cool, shaded conditions with plenty of air, because it grows mainly in the Andes. Many orchidists are having good luck under lights. Never let *M. coccinea* dry out. It will flower for months, mainly in winter and spring.

I could go on and on, relating the names of species to try and suggesting some hybrids I've had luck with. But my greatest pleasure in orchid growing has come from trying new things. I look at a strange plant and begin assessing, as any orchid grower does, how it might be cultivated. I

examine the structure of its leaves and note whether it has pseudobulbs. I ask myself: Do I like its appearance? The genus name alone often tells me a lot of general information about cultivation. If the orchid passes muster, and all too often it does, the last thing I ask is: Can I grow it?

Growing it is the challenge—and the pleasure. Among orchidists, it is said that you haven't really learned to grow a plant until you've bloomed it once yourself. Buying it in bloom doesn't count. The type of person who must always succeed may have some difficulty with orchids at first. They can be a humbling form of stress management. Many of my friends have met the challenge and quietly raise orchids that still confound me. There's always room to learn and try more.

So I try everything that comes my way, most recently a $5 oncidium (no name) from the members' sales table at my orchid society. After a year and a half, it is creeping out of a six-inch plastic pot and has its first bloom. It's a nondescript flower, I suppose, mainly brown and looking more like an epidendrum than an oncidium. There are half a dozen flowers, less than an inch wide, on a short spike.

I can probably identify my mystery oncidium now through my collection of orchid books, but I'm really in no hurry. I'm enjoying the challenge of growing the plant without knowing what it is. I do that by just getting on with growing it, mistakes and all. Careful observation of what the plant is doing usually saves me from too many disasters and allows me to exercise my philosophy of orchid growing: If it's an orchid, I want to try it.

CHAPTER NINE

The Greenhouse Effect

Finding a permanent home for your hobby.

"It is not absolutely necessary to build a house for the cultivation of orchids," wrote the eminent B.S. Williams in his Victorian cultivator's bible, *The Orchid Grower's Manual.* He was right again, of course. Greenhouses are what orchid growers get when they've run out of other places to grow their plants. That's the usual progression for most of us. As a rule of thumb, 50 indoor orchids are about all the average household can take. After exhausting the windowsills and basement growing areas, many orchidists start thinking about a greenhouse. They imagine there will suddenly be limitless space to pursue their hobby. They forget that orchid collections expand, like the universe, to overfill the allotted space. But that's a problem for later.

I, too, once stared out my back window, brooding about the unused patio space that could become a home for my orchids. If only they had a big room, full of humidity, I knew I could grow them better. I justified it in my mind long before I tried to work out whether I could afford a greenhouse. The problem was, I let the idea fester, so even when I found out the breath-stopping price of a new Lord & Burnham glass-and-aluminum greenhouse, I still had to have one.

Commercial greenhouses can be expensive, particularly when fitted with the latest gadgets for automating the structure. A hobbyist can easily spend $20,000 before the greenhouse is even stocked with plants. So when I determined I had to have my own greenhouse, there was only one way to go: build my own.

This isn't as difficult as it sounds, because a lean-to, which is what I built, can be put up safely with the most rudimentary home-handyman skills. I've done it twice now—once on the flat third-floor roof of a downtown house and once off a bedroom at ground level. Both efforts cost less than $2,000 in materials and took about

Elaborate, **above,** *or simple,* **opposite,** *a greenhouse can accommodate a growing hobby.*

Being partially buried allows better temperature control in this lean-to greenhouse, **above.**

An air conditioner, **above right,** *is necessary to keep this greenhouse cool in summer.*

Even in a greenhouse, plants can become crowded, **right.**

a week, working a few hours a day. Inspiration for the plans came from library books.

For those who don't like the home-handyman route, many builders can design and add greenhouse rooms to houses so that the growing space harmonizes delightfully with the rest of the structure. Naturally rot-resistant woods like cedar are the only kind to use in greenhouses. Pressure-treated wood contains herbicides that can harm orchids.

The first step, of course, is to choose the site for the greenhouse. Many growers opt for a greenhouse that is attached to the house, because it's easier to heat than a freestanding structure and easily links up with the electricity and water in the house.

Winter light is the major limiting factor to good growth, so the longest side of the greenhouse should face south to cut down on heating bills. A northern exposure doesn't provide enough sunlight for most orchids. The ideal orientation for a lean-to is for one side to face south and another to face east. A west-facing lean-to gets too hot in summer. On a slope, choose the highest site for the greenhouse, because cold air always settles in the lowest areas.

A greenhouse doesn't have to be on top of the ground. Underground greenhouses, where the orchids grow in a big hole covered with glass, are among the least expensive to maintain. These are very easy to keep cool during the summer months, require less heating in winter and won't detract from the look of your house.

When I considered potential sites for my first greenhouse, I found that I couldn't build on the ground. The only thing that would do was to build right on top of the house, where I had a walkout from an upper story onto a large expanse of flat roof.

For ease in building, I decided on a lean-to attached to the house. I quickly built the skeleton from cedar two-by-fours and two-by-sixes. I covered the outside with sheets of UV-resistant flat fiberglass paneling in 4-by-10-foot sheets that I tracked down through the Yellow Pages. The paneling was simply nailed to the cedar with short aluminum roofing nails, and the edges of the fiberglass were caulked.

I needed an extractor fan to remove the hot air that gathers in an enclosed light sink like a greenhouse. I installed

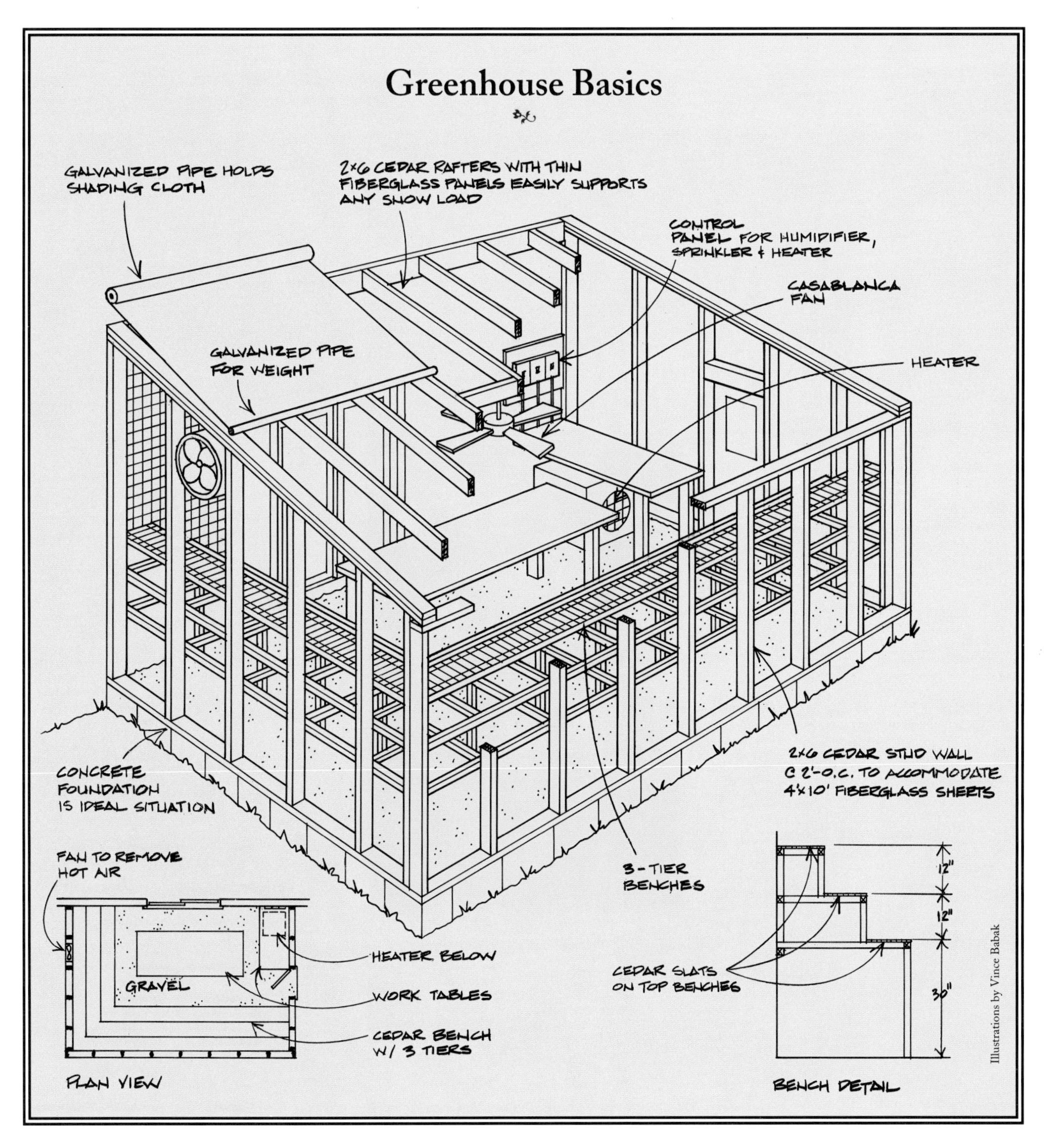

a simple squirrel-cage fan, controlled by a Penn Temperature Control A19BBC-2C. The fan automatically switches on when the temperature goes above 85 degrees F. The heater, which is controlled by a separate thermostat, switches off at 70 degrees, so there's never an accident where the heater keeps running as the fan extracts, although with the Penn control, both functions can be operated by the same device.

My heating source isn't altogether conventional for greenhouses, but it has served me well for 10 years. I use a barn, or construction, heater. Mine is an orange box about 18 inches square, which throws out 16,000 BTUs of heat, enough to keep my 10-by-20-foot lean-to above 50 degrees F on the coldest winter nights in the Northeast.

Having a fan for removing hot air in the summer is not enough, and any greenhouse that has no summer cover of shady trees requires shading cloth or blinds draped over the areas which get the most sun. This can cut down the temperature inside the greenhouse by 20 degrees.

Although some growers just spray their plants daily with a misting nozzle on the end of a hose, I think a greenhouse needs an automatic misting system.

The greenhouse needs moving air as well. The "breeze" should be strong enough so that the leaves of the orchid are visibly moving. I have a Casablanca-style fan, but some greenhouse growers use a clear plastic tube perforated with one-inch-diameter holes. When a fan is placed at one end and turned on, the tube inflates to about a foot in diameter. As the fan runs, air emerges from the holes, and little jets of mild wind are sent to various parts of the greenhouse.

The greenhouse floor ideally is made of loose stones or concrete so that it can be wet down daily by hand hosing or by a misting system installed under the benches. My greenhouse, with its jury-rigged history, has been in use for more than a decade now. Over the years, I've made adaptations as I've needed them and learned the interesting art of greenhouse growing, which can become an obsession in itself.

A greenhouse adds a huge dimension to orchid growing. Now, I can cultivate virtually any orchid I want if I set up my greenhouse to provide the right amount of heat, moisture and moving air. It's something that can't be done on the windowsill, where many orchids are restricted because of their sheer size. Here, in the Northeast, a greenhouse is a special place to be in winter. In a region where snow can blanket the ground for months, a peek into my greenhouse any time of the day or night is a tonic I don't think I'd want to live without.

A greenhouse can be cheap enough to build if you use some of my techniques, but it won't be cheap to operate. Electricity is expensive. And frankly, I've been afraid to calculate the real cost of indulging my hobby. Like the mystery-novel hero Nero Wolfe, I feel that orchid growing should not be subject to crass considerations unless abso-

A simple greenhouse can be attached to an existing sunroom.

lutely necessary. Suffice it to say that my power bill doubles in winter.

One of the advantages of a cedar greenhouse is that I can staple on an interior lining to insulate further and save on heating bills. Every year or two, in good weather, I buy a couple of rolls of 4-mil clear plastic, which I fasten to the inside of the greenhouse, covering every surface that is exposed to fiberglass. Before I begin, I tear off the old plastic, which is stained by then with water droplets and dirt. Having two layers against the outdoors holds heat in better and thus saves a lot in energy.

Once the heat, watering and air are taken care of, the important decision must be made: what to grow. By the time most orchidists get a greenhouse, they are cultivating a variety of plants. They know which orchids intrigue them, and this is the clue for setting up the greenhouse. I like to grow cattleyas, dendrobiums and oncidiums, but there are hundreds of species I haven't tried yet that are on my wish list. So I've chosen to grow in the so-called intermediate range. It allows me to try a lot of things, especially by looking for microclimates in the greenhouse.

Every structure has several microclimates, spaces often only a couple of feet square where the temperature, humidity and air movement are different. Perhaps one end of the greenhouse is cooler than the center. Here, I would put orchids in the genus *Coelogyne* or *Odontoglossum*. Or I might use it as a dry nesting area for my Indian dendrobiums. A moist area near the misters would make oncidiums and odontoglossums happy. A warm, moist area is appreciated by phalaenopsises and vandas, and there are hundreds of botanically interesting species that can live on the ground underneath the benches. Remember, the more plants you have, the higher the relative humidity, just because of the sheer square footage of green area. Orchids seem to grow better when large numbers of them are kept together.

I search for microclimates with a minimum/maximum thermometer, which I place in a likely area for a few

Once having established an orchid hobby in a greenhouse, the grower is ready to consider starting a breeding program.

days. To check local humidity, I use a little portable meter. Microclimates allow me to cultivate more kinds of orchids than I could if I chose to grow only warm or cool ranges. Now I can have some plants at both the warm and the cool ends of the family tree.

Benches are an important consideration in the layout of the greenhouse. I like to grow orchids in pots, but I also like the look of them on various pieces of wood, cork, basket and branch, where they take on their natural form, unrestricted by their city shoes.

My benches are three feet wide. The benches can either have flat surfaces or be stepped, allowing the plants to sit slightly above each other in ascending rows.

I've tried both, and for me, the stepped benches win out for ease of watering, display and general cultural worthiness, even if they are slightly more complicated to build. The plants seem to have more space on stepped benches as well. The best material for benches is hardwood slats, which also look good. They do, however, have one drawback: they attract the orchids' roots, so the plants get stuck to the benches. Wire-mesh benches don't do that.

For those who have the space, a greenhouse need not be an elaborate and expensive undertaking. The only difficult part might be convincing an incredulous life mate that what you've both wanted for a long time is a greenhouse.

Growing in a greenhouse is a radically different pursuit than growing in the house. Suddenly, the available space becomes not only home for the plants but also nursery and lab. Experiments abound, and the grower can seriously consider starting a breeding program with an eye to winning awards.

Or do as Nero Wolfe and I do: just go into your greenhouse and drink in all the sights and smells of orchids at least once a day.

CHAPTER TEN

Increasing the Bounty

An introduction to propagation techniques.

TYPICALLY, the new orchid grower goes through a number of definite stages after catching the unrelenting virus of orchid enthusiasm. One of the early stages involves acquiring more orchids. Often, any kind will do. At first, some orchidists even divide up and repot their own plants, if only to make the windowsill look less bleak. Soon enough, though, another grower will snap off a piece from a favorite clump of orchids or hand over a small potted specimen from a division, and the beginner will become one of that happy band of orchid enthusiasts: the propagators.

Propagators always have little pots of this and that to trade with fellow growers. Propagation is an excellent way to build a collection and to gain experience cultivating a variety of orchids.

The routine chore of repotting often calls for forced propagation. Every three or four years, I grit my teeth and take on the easy but tedious task of repotting one of my favorites, *Dendrobium nobile*. When an orchid grows into a big pot-filling specimen, repotting is sometimes more a matter of untangling a puzzle of roots than performing major surgery.

The plant in the picture opposite was divided into five sections by the simple expedient of making sure that each bunch of four or five canes included at least one new growth. I don't bother with the small stuff. Unless the orchid is incredibly valuable, I discard any pieces with not enough eye, or new growth, to make a good propagation. These tiny pieces invariably take years to develop into strong plants. Some never do.

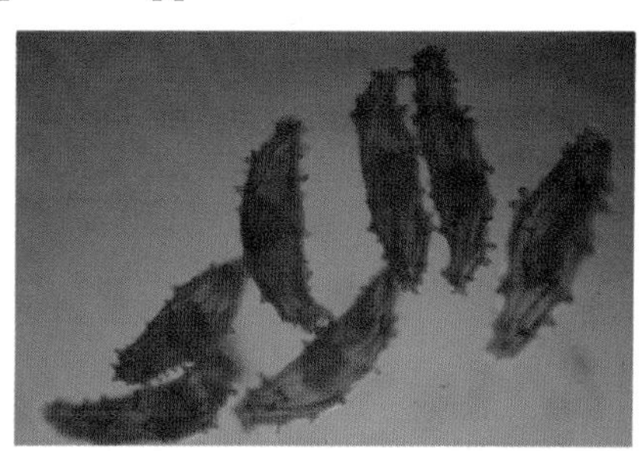

Above, ***microscopic view of catasetum seeds. A dendrobium in need of propagation,*** **opposite.**

Propagation basics, **clockwise from above.** *The author begins pulling apart a dendrobium at its natural breaking points. The old orchid yields five new plants. Potting material is pressed around the roots, but the pseudobulbs are allowed to remain above the bark.*

Don't worry if the new growth appears to be pointing the wrong way when you put it in the compost. Sunlight will right it. However, you must anchor the plant in the pot in some way so that it doesn't jiggle. If the roots of your orchid can't take hold on the inside of its container, the plant won't grow to its full potential. I usually use a rhizome clip, which can be purchased ready-made in different sizes or can be fashioned from fence wire with needle-nose pliers.

The most important consideration is that the plant does not move while the roots are growing. This may require tying it until it assumes the elegant, natural shape that makes a well-grown orchid a joy to behold. Long, green garbage-bag ties work well to secure the orchid discreetly to the post until strength returns.

Dendrobiums can also be reproduced by *keikis*, perfect plants with roots that appear at the flowering nodes when the conditions are not right for blooming. The plant may

After the new orchid has been divided and potted, a rhizome clip driven into the potting material, **right,** *ensures that the plant will stay firmly in place, even if the container is jostled.*

To create a look of neatness, the author uses twist ties to fasten loose canes to a long pot hanger, **bottom left.**

Bottom right: *The finished product, one newly potted dendrobium propagation, ready for a life on its own.*

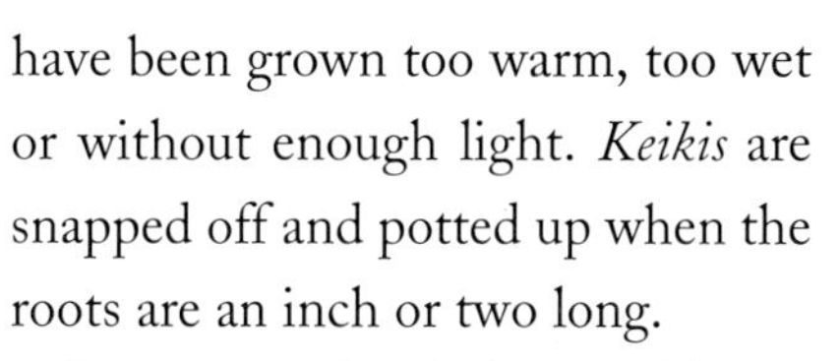

have been grown too warm, too wet or without enough light. *Keikis* are snapped off and potted up when the roots are an inch or two long.

Some cane dendrobiums, like *D. nobile*, *D. aureum*, *D. transparens*, *D. superbum* and *D. wardianum*, can be increased by taking a young but unflowered leafless cane in spring and cutting it into four-to-six-inch pieces between the nodal points. The cut-up canes are laid on a bed of moist moss, and the container is covered with glass. Within weeks, new plants will appear at the nodal points.

Propagating other orchids is sometimes as simple as placing cuttings in a compost similar to the one the

Excess water and warmth made this orchid sprout new plants, rather than flowers.

mature plant was growing in or tying the plant onto a raft of cork or a piece of native wood, like sassafras, which should be cut live so that the tight bark remains for the orchid roots to grip.

Some orchids, such as cymbidiums and cattleyas, can be propagated from seemingly lifeless back bulbs. As long as there is an eye, which can be recognized as a swelling or scale at the base of a pseudobulb, there is life. Back bulbs of odontoglossums, lycastes, dendrobiums and cymbidiums are routinely used to produce new plants. Usually the back bulb is stood on its base in a compost of fine bark, sphagnum, charcoal and perlite, mixed in a proportion of 3:1:1:1. I use a plastic mini-greenhouse with a sturdy bottom and a clear top with movable air holes. Inside this propagator, any plant "in hospital" gets almost 100 percent humidity. The warm, moist conditions encourage the emergence of dormant eyes on the back bulb. The process can take weeks or months, depending on the vigor of the back bulb and the type of orchid. As long as the back bulb remains plump and doesn't turn soft or black, the potential for new growth exists.

Monopodials, like paphiopedilums, require a slightly different approach. Some complex hybrids simply fall apart into separate growths when they are large and in need of repotting. To produce additional paphiopedilum plants, you need one old growth with a new plant emerging from between the leaves at the base. The old growth, with its few roots, nurtures the new growth until it forms its own roots. Some monopodials, like vandas, can be cut below a point where enough roots emerge from the stem to support the piece being removed. Since vandas don't grow a lot of roots, only three or four need to be buried in the compost to keep the new plant alive. If left in its pot, an old "headless" vanda will often sprout new growths.

Phalaenopsises can grow small versions of themselves along old flower stems. This frequently happens when a plant is stressed, and you will see three or four plantlets forming at the nodes of old, uncut flower spikes. The nodes can also be encouraged to produce new plants by inoculating them with a hormone paste.

Other species grow baby plants along the fat canes, which can be broken off when there are enough roots to support the new plant and potted up in a small container. There are orchids, like members of the genus *Pleione*, that throw out new versions of themselves where the last leaf has fallen from an old bulb.

Sometimes, a monopodial loses a lot of leaves from the lower section of the plant, leaving an ugly bare cane in the middle of the orchid. If there are no roots on this part of the cane, pack wet sphagnum around the bare section and cover with plastic to keep that portion of the stem moist. This encourages new roots to pop out at the mossy point. When the roots emerge, remove the sphagnum and plastic, and allow the roots to grow a couple of inches, until the plant can be cut below the new roots and repotted.

Propagating cattleyas depends on the growing style of the species. Some cattleyas branch freely, breaking two new eyes from each pseudobulb. So before long, the plant fills the pot. Other species grow in a linear fashion, forming a straight line of pseudobulbs. Branching cattleyas should be removed from the pot and cut so that there are at least four divisions with a new growth in each section. Some of the older living roots should also be present to support the plant until the new roots take over.

Cattleyas that grow in a straight line can be encouraged to branch by cutting a notch in the rhizomes just ahead of one of the leafy back bulbs you want to activate. After the cut is made, the plant is left in the pot and not disturbed until a new growth shows on one of the pseudobulbs in the rear section. If this treatment doesn't work, you haven't lost anything, because the plant will simply continue to grow straight.

Seeds and Flasks

In the mid-1800s, an orchid grower named John Dominy at Veitch's Royal Exotic Nursery, in Devon, England, succeeded in flowering the first orchid hybrid.

Orchid hybrids have given us colors and shapes that nature never intended, and although most hybrids could not survive in the wild, they have become an important part of orchid culture.

No experienced amateur seems to be able to resist trying hybridization now and then. One of my first experiments was the self-pollination of *Cattleya* species. I tried it only because the flower was there. Within days after I had pollinated it, the flower had darkened and the column had thickened and enveloped the pollen mass

Orchid Alchemy

How to concoct a homemade starting medium.

Proprietorial medium preparations are expensive and unnecessarily mysterious and complicated. Years ago, Hawaiian orchid growers discovered that a perfectly good medium could be made using simple materials.

MIX ***2 teaspoons of a concentrated, soluble plant fertilizer in a quart of water in which you have dissolved 5 to 7 level teaspoons of sugar and about 12 level teaspoons of agar, which can be obtained through your local pharmacist.***

FOR REPLATING, ***which involves moving the seedlings to another flask so they can grow bigger, the Hawaiians added half a ripe banana, mashed, to a mixture with only 8 level teaspoons of agar instead of 12. Other experiments involved mixtures containing tomato juice, pineapple juice and even fish emulsion.***

ADJUST ***the pH to about 5.0 to 5.2 with a drop or two of hydrochloric acid, available from hydroponics dealers. With this formula and some experimentation, the orchid grower can germinate most orchid seeds.***

A slight breeze carries minuscule orchid seeds aloft from a ripe pod. Millions of the fragile seeds can be released at one time, but few survive.

that I had placed on the sticky stigma. I watched the seedpod for at least six months. In that time, the pod fattened and grew to two inches in length. Then it began to turn brown and split, finally releasing a cloud of pinpoint-sized white seeds when tapped with a finger.

In their groping attempts to learn the art of reproducing these exotic plants, early orchid growers managed to cultivate a few species to maturity by sowing a dusting of orchid seeds in the pot where the mature plant was growing. The fungi that are needed to ensure germination and growth of the seeds were present in the roots and compost. If the growers were careful, they could eke out an offspring or two. No wonder orchids gained a reputation as rare and difficult plants.

All that changed in 1922, when Lewis Knudson of Cornell University discovered a way to germinate orchid seeds in an agar jelly in which sugar and nutrient chemicals were dissolved. No fungi were needed, and orchids could be germinated and grown in laboratory flasks until they were big enough to be planted in ordinary pots.

Amateur growers were quick to learn to use the technique at home. My first attempt at flasking involved boiling pots of water in my kitchen until the atmosphere literally dripped. I had previously sterilized a few jars in which I dissolved the agar nutrient solution, which can be purchased from orchid suppliers and is easy to prepare. The purpose of the steam was to drive airborne fungi to the floor, where they couldn't drop onto the agar and contaminate the nutrient when I opened the jars. The opening and seeding took place inside a cardboard box with a transparent lid. The interior of the box had been liberally swabbed with chlorine bleach, as had my instruments.

Despite my safeguards, however, three of the five flasks were covered with a fuzzy gray-and-blue fungus within a week. They were discarded.

Eighteen-month-old seedlings grow in a baby-food jar, **top.** *Orchid seedlings in flasks,* **center,** *under a grow light.* **Bottom left,** *protocorms.* **Bottom right,** *young orchids can live in a community pot for a year or more.*

The other two flasks remained clear, and a few weeks later, after sitting in subdued light at a temperature of 60 to 65 degrees F, the surface showed a dusting of green. These were protocorms that formed from the seeds. Within a year, I had more than enough orchid seedlings to wonder what I would ever have done with five flasks of germinated seeds.

Flasking is a service that a number of orchid nurseries and private individuals offer for a relatively small charge. So these days, I don't bother trying to germinate orchid seeds myself, unless I have a particularly precious pod that I won't entrust to someone else. I remember how I felt in that steamy room, wiping mist off my glasses as I tried to dust wet seeds onto the surface of the agar in the sterilized jars.

Flasks are fun to try, because they offer perhaps 50 chances at a great seedling for the price of a single mature plant. When received from the grower, the seedlings are usually ready to plant into a community pot. Just wrap the flask with a towel, then break it gently without injuring the orchids inside. The seedlings should be washed of their agar in a simple sugar solution. I like to plant the seedlings in tens in two- or three-inch plastic pots. The pots are placed in

a propagator until the seedlings are well established. I repot them as they grow larger. It can take several years for plants to grow from flask to maturity, but much can be learned about orchids along the way.

CHAPTER ELEVEN

Life Without a Home

As habitats vanish, orchids face an uncertain future in the wild.

Few orchids have caused as much of a stir in recent years as *Epidendrum ilense*. Calway Dodson, a well-known orchid researcher, found this interesting new species in the Montanas de Ilas, in the Andean foothills of Ecuador, in 1976 and described it in an orchid journal the following year.

Nothing like *Epidendrum ilense* has been seen before. Although not as showy as its cousins, the more spectacular cattleyas, *E. ilense* is unique in its pendent inflorescence with greenish white flowers clustered at the end like fringed-lipped bells. It's another of those evolutionary paths not taken, so common in nature's shotgun approach.

But *Epidendrum ilense* was worthy enough to merit additional interest. When Dodson returned to Ecuador to collect more specimens, he discovered that the unique habitat of this orchid—a small patch of jungle forest—had been cut down to make a cornfield. *E. ilense* had been snuffed out as a wild species. It has never been found in nature again.

Yct you can buy an *Epidendrum ilense* today. Luckily, Dodson brought back four specimens from the original discovery. They were grown in a greenhouse in Florida and eventually propagated clonally.

That's the dilemma for orchids today: life without a home. As more jungle is felled to make way for roads, pastures and cornfields, orchid species are fast disappearing.

***Epidendrum ilense*, above. *Epidendrum ibaguense from a Costa Rican rainforest*, opposite.**

The orchid family is so specialized in terms of its pollinators, and even the fungi which must be present in the rooting material to initiate germination of seeds, that simply cutting a tropical roadway condemns many

An Oncidium ascendens, **above,** *identical to the one seen by the author beside a Mexican river. Bees stuck in dendrobium orchids in Hawaii,* **below.**

With all the hybridizing and cloning of orchids these days, it's easy to ignore the slow attrition of many species. After all, most of the showiest orchids have been found, and those that please us can now be reproduced exactly. So there's a tendency to rush past the "weeds" of the orchid world. We do so at our peril. Any genetic orchid material will be valuable when the final cornfield has been planted.

As more hungry people set up house under the orchids' canopy and ruthless individuals exploit the trees themselves for the quick gain of a timber sale, it won't be long before orchids cease to exist in nature. And it doesn't even have to be a big event, except to a few individuals.

Nearly 20 years ago, I visited Puerto Vallarta, Mexico, shortly after the tourism explosion that followed the movie *The Night of the Iguana*. I travelled south in a rented car and soon came to a river in a gorge. I'm sure many had been there before me, but that was where I looked in fascinated wonder at my first wild orchid: an oncidium dangling upside down among pencil-shaped leaves, its tiny, butter-yellow flowers fairly glowing in the dim light of that tree branch hanging over the river. Just standing in that beautiful spot would turn even a rose fancier into an orchid grower.

I returned a few years ago and searched in vain for the spot, until I realized that it had been replaced by

species to death. With the construction of that roadway, the microclimate of an area is suddenly altered. Drier conditions are inevitable, and there is new competition from sun-loving weeds. The orchids that lived there may die out.

Researchers now know that changing the physical characteristics of an area affects all the species—plant and animal—which live there. If the pollinators disappear, orchid species can't even be reintroduced to an area that has been tampered with. The orchids that survive may live on but are unable to reproduce, so the forest becomes a kind of transient showpiece, apparently healthy, but rotten underneath.

Thelymitra ixioides, called the dotted sun orchid, growing in Australia.

a lavish restaurant filled with parrots—its theme—and two-for-one beer tickets. What I hadn't noticed on my first visit was that the riverbed where those orchids had lived happily was beautifully shaped in sandstone by centuries of water scouring so that it resembled a natural water slide with perfect stone pools. What were a few orchids, after all, when so much fun could be had drinking beer and sliding down the stone?

It would be difficult to make a case for the orchids against a better life for the farmer who once owned that piece of land. Perhaps it would be less difficult further up the economic food chain. But orchids don't vote, so most orchid growers concentrate on saving as many species as possible. That seems to be the way of the future. Growers are collecting and saving what they can against an apparently bleak future for orchid habitats.

The longer I've cultivated orchids, the more I've come to realize that we are connected to the wild places where orchids grow. My love affair with this dazzling plant family goes on because I know that out there are brothers and sisters I've never met, that no one has met. There's always the anticipation of finding a new species, like Calway Dodson did. What's most difficult to accept in the story of *Epidendrum ilense* is that many of those orchids will never be met, except by a woodcutter's chain saw.

On the other hand, orchid grow-

Epiphytic orchid (Ponthieva maculata) in a cloud forest in Costa Rica.

ing attracts such a variety of individuals that to many orchidists, the hobby always has been, and will be, a pursuit of the civilized indoor art of cultivation. A large number of growers don't cultivate natural species at all. We are in a kind of golden age of orchid hybridization at the moment. Amateurs and professionals are fashioning new genera, some of which are potentially interesting.

The jury's out, though, on the future of these hybrids. Many seem to be very difficult to grow. This is not a problem I've encountered with species. Some of the new complex hybrids have such a mix of genetic material that often only a few individuals survive flasking, and they may develop symptoms similar to those displayed by premature babies: difficulties with some physical functions, slow development and early death. Knowledgeable orchid hybridizers encourage amateurs to promote hybrid vigor by crossing back to a species, preferably one that is nearly related. That's why it is important that the connection between wild and hybrid orchids be maintained for as long as possible: their unions will be more fruitful and much better for growers.

With orchid habitats disappearing around the world, more growers are propagating their own specimens of particularly rare species. They simply take the pollen from one flower on the orchid and place it on the stigma of the same flower and wait for developments. The seeds from such unions are distributed worldwide, and species swarms are now growing in countries as widely dispersed as New Zealand and Greenland. After all, isn't this the way orchids act in nature?

Orchids dangle from the rainforest canopy in Madagascar, **above.**
A Dendrobium uncinatum grows in New Guinea, **opposite.**

My Puerto Vallarta orchid ravine no longer exists, but its memory has fueled a consciousness about orchid habitats that has made such places precious to me. It's still possible to go to a number of tropical countries for an orchid holiday, with visits and collecting trips included. Visitors inevitably come away with a sense of reverence about their experience. Just more proof, as far as I'm concerned, that this is the way we will protect our wild places in the future, by exploiting them naturally.

I am content to wave from shore as other intrepid orchid hunters embark on their collecting adventures. There is still much to be learned about orchid growing right here at home. I view the pastime with a mixture of emotions, much as I do the daughter who started it all. Despite some problems, there are many rewards—and always some surprises.

For the first time since I acquired it more than a decade ago, my *Odontoglossum pendulum* looks as if it's going to bloom. I took my own advice this spring and hung the plant in the patio in late May, leaving it outside through a couple of cold, wet weeks. The other day, I was about to brush off a twig I thought had fallen into the pot from the trees above. I stopped myself just in time, realizing that the "twig" was growing out of the newly forming green pseudobulb. It was hanging down exactly like the books say the flower spike of *Odontoglossum pendulum* should hang. I couldn't have been happier if I had been the orchid explorer who first spotted it blooming somewhere in Mexico a century ago.

Appendices

GLOSSARY

SOURCES

FURTHER READING

PHOTOGRAPHY CREDITS

INDEX

Glossary

back bulb: In sympodial orchids, the older pseudobulb behind the growing lead that has lost its leaves; used for propagation.

bifoliate: Plant bears two leaves at the top of one pseudobulb; bifoliate orchids, such as *Cattleya skinneri* and *Cattleya schilleriana*, have smaller compact flowers, with more diverse and interesting colors.

bulb: A short, vertical, underground stem for storing food materials that will be used to initiate the next growing period; includes corm, rhizome and tuber.

calyx: Collective term for the sepals of a flower, which form the outer envelope that protects the developing flower bud; usually green or greenish and leaf-like.

cleistogamous: Self-pollinating; does not rely on any external agent.

Sobralia leudoxantha,* above, *growing in a Costa Rican rainforest.* Previous pages: *Habenaria fimbriata.

column: The central sexual structure of the orchid flower, which is a long, fleshy extension formed by the fusion of stamens and pistil.

cross: The offspring of parents that are distinct varieties of the same species or are the progeny of the results of such, especially as produced through human manipulation for specific genetic characteristics; the term is sometimes applied to a hybrid between different species.

drenching: Immersing entire plant in a pesticide solution to irradicate infestation of pests.

epiphyte (from Greek *epi*, meaning "upon," and *phyton*, "a plant"): A plant that grows above ground on another plant, such as a tree, but is not parasitic on it; derives moisture and nourishment from the air and rain; also called an air plant.

eye: A growth bud, evidenced by a swelling or scale at the base of the pseudobulb.

family: A unit of classification that consists of two or more genera (but sometimes only one) considered sufficiently distinct from all other genera to warrant family recognition; the genera of which a family is composed are more closely related to each other than to other genera.

flasking: Method by which seeds can be germinated in a laboratory flask in an agar jelly in which sugar and nutrient chemicals have been dissolved; meristematic tissue can also be grown using this technique.

footcandle: A measure of light intensity; equivalent to the illumination produced by a source of one candle at a distance of one foot and equal to one lumen incident per square foot. A low reading of 1,200 footcandles is ideal for species such as *Paphiopedilum venustum*, while a reading of 8,000 footcandles would be enjoyed by some members of the Vanda family.

genus: A subdivision of a family, consisting of one or more species (sometimes thousands) that exhibit similar characteristics and appear to have a common ancestry; all of the species are discrete but closely related; a distinctive generic name (capitalized and italicized) is the first word in the scientific name or names of the species that compose it.

humidistat: A small, inexpensive gauge used for measuring and controlling the degree of humidity.

hybrid: A plant created by artificially crossing parents of different varieties, species or genera; may exhibit qualities superior to either parent; a primary hybrid is a cross between two species and is usually the most vigorous.

***keiki* (Hawaiian for "baby"):** A young orchid plantlet, complete with roots, that appears at a flowering node when conditions are not right for blooming; can be used for propagating certain species.

lead: A new vegetative growth.

lip: The modified lowermost petal of an orchid that has a distinct, often colorful appearance to attract pollinating insects; also called the labellum.

lithophyte: A plant that grows on the surface of rocks or on stony ground.

mericlone: Exact genetic copy of another plant; produced by meristem culture.

meristem: Formative tissue composed of actively dividing cells capable of dividing indefinitely and giving rise to similar cells or to cells that differentiate to produce the definitive tissues and organs; located in minute amounts within growth buds, on root tips and at the growing point of shoots.

meristem culture: Highly sophisticated method of plant propagation based on the ability of meristematic tissue to grow and develop into new individuals. Since the meristematic cells of plants infected with virus diseases are often free of viral contamination, this method of propagation can be used to establish new populations of virus-free stock. Plants raised from meristems are called mericlones.

microclimate: In a small site or habitat in a garden or greenhouse, temperature, humidity and air movement may vary significantly from those of the general region. By taking advantage of these local conditions, a grower can cultivate a wider variety of plants.

minimum/maximum thermometer: Registers the lowest and highest temperatures between settings, so grower can get an exact record of temperature variations in a specific location during a 24-hour period.

monopodial: A plant with a single stem that grows continually in one direction from the terminal shoot, year after year, adding a couple of leaves each season; has neither rhizome nor pseudobulbs.

node: A bump or joint on the stem where a leaf, flower bud or branch emerges; the stem is often slightly thickened here; can be encouraged to produce a new plant by inoculating with a hormone paste.

panicles: Branched, often loose clusters of flowers; similar to a raceme but with a branched group of flowers in place of each single flower.

petal: Modified leaf, usually brightly colored, forming part of the corolla; orchids have three petals.

pistil: The female reproductive parts of the flower that bear seeds; consists of ovary, style and stigma.

pollen: Fertilizing grains borne by the anther; in orchids, the dust-like, granular particles adhere in masses called pollinia; consists of spores that contain the male sex cells; through the process of pollination, the male cells are transported to the stigma, where fertilization occurs.

pollinator: An agent, such as an insect or the wind, that transfers pollen from one flower to another and thereby initiates pollination.

pollinia: Hardened, coherent mass of individual pollen grains often with a stalk bearing an adhesive disk that sticks to pollinators; transported as a whole during pollination; characteristic of plants such as orchids and milkweeds.

propagation: The increasing of plants by sexual or asexual means. Sexual reproduction involves pollination, the fertilization of a female egg by a male cell; the offspring usually exhibit some genetic differences from the parents. Plants produced by asexual, or vegetative, methods (i.e., taking cuttings or dividing roots or tubers), however, are essentially clones of the old ones, genetically identical.

protocorm: A tiny green ball, or tuber-like structure, that develops after an orchid seed germinates; it eventually breaks roots and becomes a true plant.

pseudobulb: The thickened bulb-like stem of an epiphytic orchid in which moisture is stored; it differs from a true bulb in that it is solid, rather than constructed of layers.

raceme: Simple arrangement of flowers on short stalks of about equal length at equal distances on a long stem; flowers open in succession toward apex.

rhizome: A modified, fleshy horizontal stem that lies on or just beneath the ground and acts as a storage organ; develops roots, leaves and flowering stems; can be used to propagate the plant.

rhizome clip: A device fashioned from wire bent into the shape of a capital T (looks somewhat like the handle and stem of a corkscrew), with a hook at one end that clips onto the side of the pot and a horizontal arm that exerts pressure on the surface of the plant in the potting medium; used to secure a newly potted plant so that it won't jiggle and the roots can take hold.

salep: The starchy, mucilaginous tubers of various orchids, especially the genus *Orchis*, that are dried, then ground into a powder to be used for food and medicine.

scape: A stalk emerging from the base of the plant that bears flowers, rather than leaves.

sepal: One of the small leaf-like segments of the calyx, or outer ring of flower parts, that protect the developing flower bud; usually green or greenish, but sometimes colored and petal-like; orchids have three sepals.

sheath: A tubular protective envelope that develops at the base of the leaf and enfolds the stem.

species: Any of the taxonomic groups into which a genus is divided, the members of which resemble one another and consistently breed true; in the scientific name, the species appears as the second word (lowercase and italicized).

species swarms: Remote colonies of orchids that evolve to suit the habitat when seeds are carried great distances from their place of origin; this accounts for the huge variety of orchid species.

spike: A flower stem in which the individual blossoms have no stalk; emerges from the base of the most newly mature bulb after initiation of dry, cool conditions.

stamen: The male reproductive organ of the flower that bears pollen; consists of a filament and anther.

stigma: The enlarged tip of the pistil, or female organ of the flower, that is receptive to pollen.

sympodial: A plant that sends out a new shoot from the rhizome of the previous growth that is a complete plant in itself; a number of lateral branches emerge from just behind the apex of the main stem, which ceases to grow; the bases of the branches are frequently developed as pseudobulbs; when the branches reach a certain length, they stop growing; what looks like a simple stem is made up of the bases of several stems that arise successively as branches, one from another.

terrestrial: Growing in the earth or on the ground, as distinct from epiphytic or lithophytic.

tribe: A group of related genera; a subdivision of a subfamily.

tuber: A swollen, fleshy underground stem used for food storage, with eyes or buds from which new plants may arise.

unifoliate: Plant bears a single leaf on a club-shaped pseudobulb (*Cattleya labiata*; *Cattleya trianaei*).

variety: A subdivision of a species; does not apply to hybrids; usually fertile with other members of the species to which it belongs but differs from the species in general in at least one reproducible quality; indicated by third word of scientific name.

velamen: Thick, spongy outer layer of cells on the roots of epiphytic orchids that absorbs moisture from the surroundings.

virus: Submicroscopic infective agent that can reproduce only inside the living cells of plants and animals; responsible for causing several serious plant diseases; can be spread by insects and other creatures, tools and even (especially with tobacco mosaic virus) by handling healthy plants after touching infected ones; symptoms include weaker plants with mosaic patterns on their leaves, often circled by rings of brown, and smaller flowers that are streaked.

Sources

Those infected with the gardening spirit are not, by instinct, joiners and meeting goers: growing things for pleasure, especially when one is still an unsure beginner, is hardly a team sport.

Nevertheless, for those contemplating a plunge into orchids, there's no better place to start than by becoming a member of the American Orchid Society (AOS). If this sounds like joining the Royal Yacht Club before you've bought your first dinghy, the immediate benefit for neophyte orchidists in belonging to the AOS is access to its indispensable monthly magazine.

The *AOS Bulletin* is simply the best opportunity to see what's happening in the orchid world and, in my opinion, is easily the finest specialized garden-society magazine I've ever encountered, with excellent photographs and informative articles. The advertisements at the back of the magazine were my first sources for many orchid supplies, since growers from all over North America are listed. There are often monthly specials, and even a look at the

Phalaenopsis amboinensis, **above,** ***is an Indonesian orchid that can be grown by home hobbyists.***

advertisements will give you a sense of what's happening in the Orchid World. It sometimes helps to mention being an AOS member when dealing with mail-order orchid suppliers, and members may buy orchid books from the AOS at a discount.

Membership, including an annual subscription to the magazine, is $30 a year ($36 outside the United States). The *AOS Bulletin* can open the door to the fascinating world of orchid growers and suppliers, and even one year's subscription is worth the price to develop a sense of the variety of plants and equipment available to enthusiasts. Write:

American Orchid Society
6000 South Olive Avenue
West Palm Beach, FL 33405
Office: 407-585-8666; Book Services: 405-585-2510; Fax: 407-585-0654

There are also a number of smaller specialized societies, such as the Cymbidium Society of America or the Phalaenopsis Guild, with many benefits for those who have narrowed their interests to a certain genus of orchids.

In Britain write:

Orchid Society of Great Britain
120 Crofton Road
Orpington, Kent BR6 8HZ
United Kingdom

British Orchid Council
20 Newbury Drive
Davyhulme, Manchester M31 2FA
United Kingdom

The AOS publishes the *AOS Almanac*, listing orchid societies and many orchid wholesalers and retailers. This plump booklet can direct you to the nearest orchid society, where you should be able to get the names of otherwise hard-to-find small local dealers. Soon, you'll be finding orchidists where you least expect them.

The following is a totally arbitrary list of mail-order sources with reputations for good quality and reliable service. It is not intended to endorse any of the firms to the exclusion of others.

Mail-Order Growers & Suppliers

The Angraecum House
P.O. Box 976
Grass Valley, CA 95945
916-273-9426

Here is an essential source for growers interested in African orchids, particularly *Angraecum* species, owner Fred Hillerman's lifelong obsession. A huge variety of unusual species and hybrids is available.

Bergstrom Orchids
494 Camino Manzanas
Thousand Oaks, CA 91360
805-495-1792
Fax: 805-379-4522

Bergstrom Orchids is one of the mail-order standbys, and I like its intriguing advertisements for oddball species, like this one: "*Trigonidium egertonianum*. This is that very interesting species with the quaint appearance of open lapels on an expensive suit. Ready to bloom. $10." U.S. orders only.

Carmela Orchids
P.O. Box H
Hakalau, Hawaii 96710
808-963-6189
Fax: 808-963-6125

For *Phalaenopsis* species, here is a Hawaiian source with good prices, excellent quality and the latest hybrids. You can try community pots of Phals for $25 if you want to wet your feet in the world of club judging for ribbons. This is also a good place to get miniature cattleyas, the popular windowsill and underlights hybrids.

Clargreen Gardens
814 Southdown Road
Mississauga, Ontario L5J 2Y4
Canada
416-822-0992
Fax: 416-822-7282

There are a number of large and small orchid growers around Toronto, where I live, but one of the biggest is Clargreen Gardens. The folks here are involved in some modest breeding programs, and tropical plants of all sizes are available in the extensive greenhouse. I browse here regularly, because it gives me a chance to wander in someone else's greenhouse for a change. Ask for a tour of the big orchid greenhouse that is not normally open to the public. A good source of supplies for Canadian growers.

Fordyce Orchids
1330 Isabel Avenue
Livermore, CA 94550
415-828-3211 or 415-447-7171 (nursery)
Fax: 415-828-3211

Frank Fordyce is one of the great names in miniature-cattleya breeding, and his nursery is definitely worth a visit for those in the San Francisco area.

J & L Orchids
20 Sherwood Road
Easton, CT 06612
203-261-3772
Fax: 203-261-8730

In the Northeast, J & L Orchids is a helpful, well-stocked source for species and hybrids of cool-growing orchids. J & L always displays an interesting collection of odontoglossums, oncidiums, masdevallias and sundry other chilly-climate specimens at my orchid society's big spring show.

Kawamoto Orchid Nursery
2630 Waiomao Road
Honolulu, HI 96816
808-732-5808
Fax: 808-732-5572

For an orchid grower, a visit to Kawamoto Orchid Nursery can be the highlight of a trip to Waikiki. Everything from dendrobiums to vandas to unusual Asian cattleyas and miniature cattleyas. Call for exact directions.

Krull-Smith Orchids
2815 Ponkan Road
Apopka, FL 32712
407-886-0915
Fax: 407-886-0438

If you're in the Disney World area of Florida, telephone for an appointment to visit Krull-Smith Orchids. You will find an interesting and varied collection of *Phalaenopsis* and *Paphiopedilum* species as well as other orchids. Flasking service.

Oak Hill Gardens
37W550 Binnie Road
W. Dundee, IL 60118
708-428-8500

When in the Chicago area, drop in and see Hermann Pigors at Oak Hill Gardens. He's not far from Chicago O'Hare International Airport and always seems happy to talk about growing *Cymbidium* and *Cattleya* species. A catalog is available.

Orchid World International
10885 S.W. 95th Street
Miami, FL 33176
800-367-6720 or 305-271-0268

Here is a well-known source offering a variety of mericlones and seedlings of warm-to-intermediate-climate growers. It will ship plants in bud for holiday giving and, if requested, will include basic growing instructions.

Orchids by Hausermann
2N134 Addison Road
Villa Park, IL 60181-1191
708-543-6855
Fax: 708-543-9842

When I first started in orchids, Hausermann sent me a picture-filled catalog that I found invaluable in making mail-order choices. This catalog is free to AOS members. Hausermann has a huge stock of orchids, claiming 190 varieties of *Cattleya* mericlones alone. This is a good place to visit just to see orchids growing. The staff leaves you alone to explore the great varieties of plants offered. The store also carries books and orchid supplies.

R.J. Rands Orchids
421 Westlake Blvd.
Malibu, CA 90265
818-707-3410

For any species of *Paphiopedilum*, real or imagined, R.J. Rands is the place to try. It has dealt exclusively in paphiopedilums and phragmipediums as well as primary hybrids for years. It was here that I got some of my early specimens of Paphs and Phrags. It ships plants in pots for less root disturbance. The range is open by appointment only.

The Rod McLellan Company
1450 El Camino Real
South San Francisco, CA 94080
800-237-4089 or 415-871-5655
Fax: 415-871-2806

McLellan has been in the orchid business for more than 50 years. It is a good West Coast source of *Cymbidium* and *Cattleya* species and has a large stock of supplies.

Tropical Plant Products, Inc.
P.O. Box 547754
Orlando, FL 32854-7754
407-293-2451

For hard-to-obtain supplies like coconut-husk fiber, osmunda, tree fern and redwood bark, Tropical Plant Products is just a UPS shipment away. A stamped, self-addressed envelope brings a free price list.

Zuma Canyon Orchids
5949 Bonsall Drive
Malibu, CA 90265
213-457-9771
Fax: 213-457-4783

George Vasquez has been a continuing pioneer in *Phalaenopsis* breeding for as long as I can remember, even before Zuma Canyon took its present name. I have several of his crosses in my collection and love them all.

ORDERING

Although some growers will ask for payment by check or money order, most prefer to handle telephone orders for orchids by credit card. Remember when ordering from other countries that some government paperwork is required for health reasons and because of the international agreement known as CITES (Convention on International Trade in Endangered Species of Wild Fauna and Flora).

PLANT-GROWTH REGULATORS

Plant Hormones Canada
Dr. James D. Brasch
2100 Highview Drive
Burlington, Ontario L7R 3X4
Canada
416-335-1713

Although your local garden center is not likely to carry them, a number of plant-growth regulators have been tried on orchids, with varying degrees of success. One of the easiest for the amateur to use is Keikigrow Plus, which contains hormones and vitamins that can help stimulate the growth of plantlets on *Phalaenopsis* and other genera. Also available from Dr. Brasch is a hormone preparation to stimulate root growth, a dormant-bud stimulant and a salve that is said to stop crown rot in Phals.

PREMIXED MOTHER FLASK MEDIA

Chemicals and equipment needed to germinate your own orchid seeds are available from:

G & S Laboratories
645 Stoddard Lane
Santa Barbara, CA 93108
805-969-5991

Sigma Chemical Company
P.O. Box 14508
St. Louis, MO 63178
314-771-5765

G & B Orchid Laboratory
2426 Cherimoya Drive
Vista, CA 92084
619-727-2611

(G & B also sells agar and mineral salts separately, so you can mix your own special formulas.)

Further Reading

READING is a key part of any orchid grower's repertoire. I browse in used bookstores, looking for old or out-of-print orchid books. Surprising nuggets of knowledge can be found between their covers, and I've spent more than one sleepless night with a stack of newly acquired orchid books, counting blossoms instead of sheep.

Here are some of my personal favorites, many of which are available through the AOS Book Services or book dealers specializing in rare, used and new orchid books, such as McQuerry Orchid Books, 5700 W. Salerno Road, Jacksonville, FL 32244 (904-387-5044).

Home Orchid Growing
Rebecca Tyson Northen
Prentice-Hall; 4th edition, 1990
$45

Rebecca Tyson Northen has been an inspiration to aspiring orchid growers for decades, and this is one orchid book for every beginner's library. It has been revised several times since it was first printed in 1950 and has become

With an interesting fan shape, Cirrhopetalum amesianum,* above, *is a native of Malaysia.

an admirable reference for almost every aspect of orchid growing. The latest edition reflects on many of the major changes in orchid names over the past two decades.

Northen's list of species and their characteristics provided my first acquaintance with the hurly-burly world of orchid nomenclature. Her concise description of each group has helped me decode and correct many of the orchid tags I've encountered. There are excellent sections that give a good grounding in the major orchid families as well as step-by-step hints for doing your own flasking, a pest and control section and a collector's section with brief descriptions of many of the rarer orchids for the grower who must have more than the obvious.

Northen writes with an easy, informative grace that I found very helpful in my early orchid days. My own copy of her book is now jacketless, bent and marked with stains, surely the best recommendation possible.

Miniature Orchids

Rebecca Tyson Northen
Prentice-Hall; 1988
$19.95

A specialized companion to Northen's *Home Orchid Growing*, this classic lists more than 600 miniature species, many suitable for the window or under-lights grower. Although the book could use some updating, with more color photographs, the text, as always in Northen's case, is clear and helpful. A good one for your collection. Available from the AOS.

Orchid Growing Illustrated

Brian & Wilma Rittershausen
Stirling Publishing; 1985
$29.95

This book stands out because of its wonderful illustrations. Photographs are both black and white and color, with excellent views of important things like roots, propagation and potting techniques. The section on pests has detailed renderings of spider mite damage and control techniques for some of the more loathsome diseases, such as the various wilts and rots that sometimes beset orchids. Highly recommended for growers whose orchids have developed a problem they've never seen before. I like it for its nonthreatening advice.

Orchids: Care and Cultivation

Gérald Leroy-Terquem & Jean Parisot
Blandford; 1991
$24.95

Here, the reader is in store for a bit of flag-waving, but the French do have much to boast about in orchid growing. This is an excellent beginner's book on all important aspects of orchid cultivation, with helpful, modern illustrations in glorious color. It is directed mostly at growing orchids in a greenhouse but is full of useful insights for all levels of amateur growers.

Orchids for Everyone

Brian Williams, et al.
Crown Publishers; 1980
Out of Print

This excellent British book is full of information on all aspects of orchid growing, particularly in the greenhouse. Many appealing illustrations and large dollops of sound advice that can be adapted for growers in any part of the world.

The Orchid Doctor

R.M. Hamilton
Self-published; 1980
$18

This useful book gives quick references to problems and cures for a variety of orchid conditions. Available from the AOS.

Handbook on Orchid Nomenclature and Registration

International Orchid Commission; 1985
$6.50

A basic reference book to all orchids and what to call them. If you're a hybridizer and your toothpick has been straying among the flowers, this is the official guide to naming your cross, no matter how odd the marriage. Available from the AOS.

Creating Oncidiinae Intergenerics

M.A. & W.W. Goodale Moir

University of Hawaii Press; 1982
$12
Available from the AOS.

Laeliinae Intergenerics
M.A. & W.W. Goodale Moir
University of Hawaii Press; 1982
$12

Goodale Moir was a remarkable hybridist, responsible for many wild and wonderful intergenerics produced with the help of his wife May. Even if you aren't particularly interested in orchid breeding, you will be held by Moir's style. In a strangely hypnotic fashion, he combines facts, opinions, chromosome counts and advice on how to produce quality hybrids. An excellent demonstration of the orchid mind at work.

Encyclopedia of Cultivated Orchids
Alex Hawkes
American International; reprinted 1987
$100

This is a quirky sort of book for more advanced orchid students. Although not really up to date, it is full of unusual and interesting species and oddball references. Available from the AOS.

Orchid Hunting in the Lost World (and Elsewhere in Venezuela)
G.C. & E. Dunsterville
American Orchid Society; 1988
$30

These are charming memoirs of a lifetime of hunting and growing orchids in South America by two American expatriates. For years, the Dunstervilles kept readers of the *AOS Bulletin* in touch with their exploits in the wilds of Venezuela. The accompanying photographs depict orchids most of us can only ever dream of seeing.

Videos

The AOS also sells videocassettes ($29.95 each) on various aspects of orchid growing, including potting, controlling pests and growing orchids under lights.

Photography Credits

Cover: Scott Camazine

Front of Book

page 2, Charles Marden Fitch; page 6-7, DRK/Pat O'Hara; page 4-5, Mark Webb; page 8-9, Scott Camazine

Chapter One

page 10, DRK/Pat O'Hara; page 11, Alain Masson; page 12, bottom, Charles Marden Fitch; page 12, top, DRK/Michael Fogden; page 13, top, Bettman Archive; page 13, bottom, DRK/Stephen J. Krasemann; page 14, Kjell Sandved; page 15, Kjell Sandved

Chapter Two

page 16, Charles Marden Fitch; page 17, DRK/Stephen J. Krasemann; page 18, top, DRK/ Michael Fogden ; page 18, bottom left, Kjell Sandved; page 18, bottom right, DRK/Michael Fogden; page 19, bottom right, Charles Marden Fitch; page 19, top left, Charles Marden Fitch; page 20, DRK/Stephen J. Krasemann; page 21, bottom left and right, Charles Marden Fitch; page 21, top left, Scott Camazine; page 22, Connie Toops; page 23, Courtesy of Hunt Institute for Botanical Documentation, Carnegie Mellon University, Pittsburgh, PA

The striking Schomburgkia orchid,* above, *grows wild in central and northern South America.

Chapter Three

page 24, Charles Marden Fitch; page 25, Charles Marden Fitch; page 26, bottom left and right, Alain Masson; page 26, top, Connie Toops; page 27, Alain Masson; page 28-29, Charles Marden Fitch; page 30, all, Alain Masson; page 31, all, Charles Marden Fitch

Chapter Four

page 32, Scott Camazine; page 33, Kjell Sandved; page 34, Alain Masson; page 35, bottom left and top left, Charles Marden Fitch; page 35, bottom right, Connie Toops; page 35, top right, Kjell Sandved; page 36, Scott Camazine; page 37, Kjell Sandved; page 38, Profiles West/L.J. Tinstman; page 39, Phil Matt; page 40, Charles Marden Fitch; page 41, bottom right, Charles Marden Fitch; page 41, top left, Alain Masson

Chapter Five

page 42, Scott Camazine; page 43, Andrew Brown; page 44, Alain Masson; page 45, bottom, Charles Marden Fitch; page 45, top, Courtesy of Hunt Institute for Botanical Documentation, Carnegie Mellon University, Pittsburgh, PA; page 46, bottom, Charles Marden Fitch; page 46, top, Alain Masson; page 48, left and bottom right, Alain Masson; page 48, top right, Charles Marden Fitch; page 49, Scott Camazine

Chapter Six

page 50, Alain Masson; page 51, Charles Marden Fitch; page 52, all except bottom right, Alain Masson; bottom right, Charles Marden Fitch; page 53, Charles Marden Fitch; page 54, first row, bottom, Alain Masson; page 54, all, Alain Masson; page 55, Alain Masson; page 56, DRK/Belinda Wright; page 57, Alain Masson

Chapter Seven

page 58, Alain Masson; page 59, Alain Masson; page 60, Kjell Sandved; page 61, all, Alain Masson; page 62, Charles Marden Fitch; page 63, all except bottom left and top left, Charles Marden Fitch; page 63, bottom left, Animals Animals/Earth Scenes; page 63, top left, Scott Camazine; page 66, Alain Masson; page 67, Scott Camazine

Chapter Eight

page 68, Charles Marden Fitch; page 69, Charles Marden Fitch; page 70, bottom right, Charles Marden Fitch; page 70, left, Kjell Sandved; page 70, top right, Alain Masson; page 71, Scott Camazine; page 72, Charles Marden Fitch; page 73, bottom, Kjell Sandved; page 73, top, Profiles West/L.J. Tinstman; page 74, Alain Masson; page 75, Kjell Sandved; page 76, Charles Marden Fitch; page 77, bottom, Charles Marden Fitch; page 77, top, Kjell Sandved; page 78, Mark Webb; page 79, Alain Masson; page 80-81, Mark Webb; page 82, Scott Camazine; page 83, bottom, Dency Kane; page 83, top, Kjell Sandved; page 84, Profiles West/ Tomas del Amo; page 85, bottom, Charles Marden Fitch; page 85, top right, DRK/D. Cavagnaro; page 85, top left, Visuals Unlimited/R. Gustafson; page 86, Jim Brandenburg/Minden Pictures; page 87, left, Alain Masson; page 87, right, Visuals Unlimited/George Loun; page 88, Kjell Sandved; page 89, Alain Masson; page 90, Kjell Sandved; page 91, bottom left, Kjell Sandved; page 91, bottom right and top, Scott Camazine; page 92, Charles Marden Fitch; page 93, Scott Camazine; page 94, Kjell Sandved; page 95, Kjell Sandved; page 96, Kjell Sandved; page 97, Profiles West/L. J. Tinstman; page 98, Comstock/Michael S. Thompson; page 99, Scott Camazine; page 100, Kjell Sandved; page 101, Kjell Sandved

Chapter Nine

page 102, Alain Masson; page 103, Phil Matt; page 104, all, Alain Masson; page 106, Alain Masson; page 107, Charles Marden Fitch

Chapter Ten

page 108, Alain Masson; page 109, Charles Marden Fitch; page 110, all, Alain Masson; page 111, all, Alain Masson; page 112, Alain Masson; page 113, Alain Masson; page 114, Charles Marden Fitch; page 115, bottom left and bottom right, Scott Camazine; page 115, middle, Alain Masson; page 115, top, Charles Marden Fitch;

Chapter Eleven

page 116, DRK /Stephen J. Krasemann; page 117, Mark Webb; page 118, bottom, Kjell Sandved; page 118, top, DRK/C.C. Lockwood; page 119, Mark Webb; page 120-121, DRK/Michael Fogden; page 122, Kjell Sandved; page 123, Frans Lanting/Minden Pictures

Appendices

page 124-125, DRK/Barbara Gerlach; page 126, DRK/Stephen J. Krasemann; page 130, Charles Marden Fitch; page 134, Kjell Sandved; page 137, Kjell Sandved; page 139, Dency Kane

Index

Cymbidiums,* above, *are among the many orchid groups accessible to novice growers.

Aerides, 98
air circulation, 44, 49. *See also* Fans
American Orchid Society, 40, 131
Angraecum sesquipedale, 100
  photo, 11
  x *A. eburneum*, photo, 99
Ansellia nilotica, 100
  photo, 100
aquariums for orchid growing, 44
Arachnis, 98
Ascocentrum, 98
Aspasia, 91

back bulb
  definition, 126
  propagation from, 112
bacterial diseases, 65
Banks, Joseph, 13
Beallara, 91
benches in the greenhouse, 107
Benlate DF, 44
bifoliate, definition, 126
Bletilla, 60
blooming after time outdoors, 60
Brassavola, 70
  digbyana, 70-71, 76; photo, 72
  nodosa, 75
Brassia, 91
  cultivation, 95
  gireoudiana, 95
  verrucosa, photo, 95
Brassocattleya, 71

Binosa, 75
Brassolaeliocattleya, 71
photo, 19
Broughtonia, 70
bulb, definition, 126
Bulbophyllum, 100
barbigerum, photo, 101

Calanthe vestita, 100
Calypso, photo, 6-7
calyx, definition, 126
Catasetum, 47, 48
cultivation, 96-97
photo, 18
seeds, photo, 109
fimbriatum, photo, 96
macrocarpum, 97
pileatum, 97
Cattleya, 40, 44, 106
as a beginner's plant, 37, 38
cultivation, 70-76
light requirements, 47, 48
photos, 21, 37, 48, 49, 58, 66
potting mix for, 56
propagation from back bulbs, 112
reproduction, 20
self-pollination of, 113-114
aclandiae, 70
amethystoglossa, 70
aurantiaca, 73-74; photo, 73
bicolor, 75; photo, 68
bowringiana, 74
Chocolate Drop 'Kodama' AM/AOS, 65, 66, 74; photo, 74
dowiana var. *aurea*, 70
forbesii, 74; photo, 73
guttata var. *Leopoldii*, 74
labiata, 70; photo, 71
leopoldii, 38
schilleriana, 70
skinneri, 70, 74; photo, 70
Small World, photo, 70
trianaei, 70
charcoal, 54, 55, 56
Cirrhopetalum amesianum, photo, 134
cleistogamous
definition, 126
orchids, 18
Cochlioda, 91
coconut fiber, 55
Coelogyne, 106
column, definition, 127
Cook, Captain James, 13
illus., 13
cool-temperature orchids, 60
cork
nuggets, 54
slab, 54
wine, 54; photo, 55
Coryanthes, 18, 96
cross, definition, 127
cultivation, 25-31
history of, 13-15
requirements, 21-23, 27-30, 43-49
Cycnoches, 96
chlorochilon, 97
Cymbidium, 37, 47, 60, 93, 112
cultivation, 82-85
miniature, 82-83
photos, 42, 139
viruses, 65
Alexanderi 'Westonbirt,' 82
dayanum, 83
devonianum, 83, 85
eburneum, 85
elegans, 83
ensifolium, 83
Nathaniel, photo, 83
pumilum, 83
tigrinum, 83; photo, 83
tracyanum, photo, 10
Velvet Fire, photo, 82
Cypripedium, 60, 87
calceolus, photo, 86
reginae, 18. *See also* Lady's-slipper

Dendrobium, 44, 48, 60, 61, 106
cultivation, 77-81
deciduous, 78-79
division of, photos, 110-111
evergreen, 77-78
photos, 52, 66, 108, 118
aggregatum, 79; photo, 77
antennatum, 77
aureum, 111
chrysanthum, 79
cuthbertsonii, photo, 4-5
densiflorum, 80; photo, 13
findlayanum, 79
heterocarpum, 79
kingianum, 79-80
moschatum, 79
nobile, 33, 78-79, 109, 111
parishii, 79
phalaenopsis, 77, 78; photos, 12, 77
pierardii, 79, 80; photo, 78
senile, 77
speciosum, 79
spectabile, 80; photo, 80-81
superbum, 111
transparens, 111
uncinatum, 122
wardianum, 79, 111
desiccated plants, reviving, 79
Diacrium, 70
bicornutum, 76; photo, 76
diazinon, 63
diseases, 65-66
division of plants, 109-113
Dodson, Calway, 117
Dominy, John, 113
Doritaenopsis, 86
Doritis pulcherrima, 86
drenching, definition, 127
dry season, 21

Epidendrum, 76
illus., 23
alatum, 76
atropurpureum, 76; photo, 75
ciliare, photo, 17
fragrans, 33-34; photo, 33
ibaguense, photos, 62, 116
ilense, 117, 121; photo, 117
pseudepidendrum, 76
epiphyte, 19-20
definition, 127
eye, definition, 127

family, definition, 127
fans, 44. *See also* Air circulation
greenhouse, 104-105, 106
fertilizing, 49
phalaenopsis, 27
finding orchids, 39-41
fir bark, 54, 55, 56
fish emulsion, 49
flasking, 114-115
definition, 127
fluorescent lights, 46-47

footcandle
calculation of, 27
definition, 127
fox tail orchid, photo, 56
fungal diseases, 44, 65
fungus gnats, 63

genus, definition, 127
germinating orchid seeds, 113-115
golden chain orchid, photo, 14
Gongora, 96
greenhouses, 103-107
construction details, illus., 105
orientation of, 104
underground, 104
window, 44-45
growing lights, 45-49
growing orchids from seed, 113-115
growth patterns, 19-20, 21
growth regulators, source, 133

Habenaria fimbriata, photo, 124
habitat, destruction of, 117-123
halide lights, 47-48
Handbook on Orchid Pests and Diseases, 66
heating the greenhouse, 104-105
helmet orchid, 18
hormone paste, 112
humidifier, mist, 45
humidistat, 27-28
definition, 127
humidity
and pests, 61-63
raising, 44
requirements, 23, 43
requirements, phalaenopsis, 27-28
trays, 45
hybrid
definition, 127
orchids, names, 34

insulation in the greenhouse, 106

keiki, 79
definition, 127
propagation from, 110-111
Kelthane, 63
Knudson, Lewis, 114

lady's-slipper, 18, 60, 87
photo, 20
Laelia, 37, 70, 71
photo, 51
anceps, photo, 35
autumnalis, 75
gouldiana, 75
purpurata, 75
Laeliocattleya, 71
Culminant 'La Tuilerie,' 74-75
Winter Ruby, photo, 70
lath house, 67
construction details, illus., 64
lead, definition, 127
light
artificial, 45-48
requirements, 21-23, 43
requirements, phalaenopsis, 27
and temperature, 48-49
timing of, 47
light stands, construction details, illus., 47
photo, 46
Linden, Jean, 15
lip, definition, 127
lithophyte, definition, 127
Lycaste, 60, 112
aromatica, 100

mail order
purchases, 39, 40
sources, 131-133
malathion, 63
Masdevallia, 37, 40, 60
Angel Frost, photo, 35
coccinea, 100
militaris, photo, 15
Maxillaria bicolor, 19
mealybugs, 60, 63
and humidity, 63
media
potting, 53-57
seed-starting, 113
seed-starting, sources, 133
mericlone, 38-39
definition, 127
meristem, definition, 127
meristem culture, 38-39
definition, 127-128
metal halide lights, 47-48
microclimate
definition, 128
in the greenhouse, 106-107
Milton, Viscount, 93
Miltonia, 91, 92
Andean, 93, 95
Brazilian, 93, 95
cultivation, 93-95
photo, 52
Bluntii, 95
clowesii, photo, 94
flavescens, 95
Lycaena 'Stamperland' FCC/RHS, 95
Miltoniopsis, 60
Bert Field 'Crimson Glow,' photo, 93
minicatt, 73
photo, 70
minimum/maximum thermometer, 45, 106-107
definition, 128
photo, 46
misting system, 106
monopodial
definition, 128
orchids, 20, 21
propagation of, 112-113
Morel, Georges, 39
Mormodes, 96
moth orchid, 25. *See also Phalaenopsis*

names of orchids, 34
pronunciation, 38
New Zealand sphagnum, 54, 55-56
node, definition, 128

Odontoglossum, 36, 91, 92, 95
cultivation, 92-93
photo, 35
propagation from back bulbs, 112
temperature requirements, 60, 106
bictoniense, 93; photo, 92
cervantesii, photo, 60
citrosmum, 67
crispum, 93
grande, 93
pendulum, 23, 67, 123
pulchellum, 93
Oncidium, 23, 118
cultivation, 91-92
humidity requirements, 106

light requirements, 47, 48
photos, 50, 61
temperature requirements, 60
altissimum, photo, 22
ampliatum, 92; photo, 91
ascendens, photo, 118
flexuosum, 92
henekenii, photo, 91
Magic Touch, photo, 91
splendidum, 92
orchids
biology, 17-21
evaluation of, 41
growing, reasons for, 11-15
growth patterns, 19-20, 21
history of cultivation, 13-15
names, 34, 38
reproduction, 18-21
seasons, 21
societies, 40, 131
societies as plant sources, 40-41
societies, value of, 12-13
species, great variety of, 19, 25
wild, habitat destruction, 117-123
wild, importance, of, 123
Orchis, 17
osmunda, 54, 55
outdoor orchid growing, 59-60, 66-67
overwatering. *See* Watering, excessive

panicles, definition, 128
pansy orchid, 93
Paphiopedilum, 18, 20, 33, 44
as a beginner's plant, 37, 39
cultivation, 87-90
light requirements, 48
photos, 19, 32
potting mix for, 56
propagation, 112
temperature requirements, 60
armeniacum, 88; photo, 87
bellatulum, photo, 8-9
fairieanum, 39, 40; photo, 87
glaucophyllum, 90
hirsutissimum, 39, 89-90; photo, 89
insigne, 39, 90
primulinum, 90
purpuratum, 90
spiceranum, 39
venustum, 88, 89; photo, 88
peat moss, 56
perlite, 54, 55, 56
pests and diseases, 60-66
petal, definition, 128
Phalaenopsis, 40, 56, 98
as a beginner's plant, 37
blooming time, 26, 30
cultivation, 25-31, 85-86
light requirements, 48
photos, 24, 25, 36-37, 52, 57, 61
propagation, 112
and spider mites, 61
temperature and humidity requirements, 106
Agus Ligo 'TC,' photo, 28-29
amabilis, 85; photo, 84
amboinensis, photo, 130
gigantea, 85
hieroglyphica, 86
Linda Miller 'Talisman Cove,' photo, 31
lueddemanniana, 26, 86; photos, 26, 85
lueddemanniana var. *ochracea*, 86
mariae, 86
schilleriana, 86; photo, 85
stuartiana, 86
violacea, 85; photo, 16
Phragmipedium, 60, 87
cultivation, 90-91
Grande, 35; photo, 90
Grande 'Beau Geste,' photo, 35
Sedenii, 90-91
pistil, definition, 128
Pleione, 113
Pleurothallis, 60
photo, 18
pollen, definition, 128
pollination, 18
pollinator, definition, 128
pollinia, definition, 128
Ponthieva maculata, photo, 120-121
pots, types, 51
potting, 51-57
hints, 53
materials, 53-57
mixes, 55-57
phalaenopsis, 30-31
pronunciation of names, 38
propagation. *See also* Meristem culture
definition, 128
from seed, 113-115
techniques, 109-115
propagator, 112
protection for outdoor orchids, 60
protocorm, 19
definition, 128
photo, 115
pseudobulb, 20-21
definition, 128
photo, 21
purchasing orchids, 26, 39-41

raceme, definition, 128
Renanthera, 98
repotting. *See* Potting
reproduction, 18-21. *See also* Meristem culture; Propagation
reviving desiccated orchids, 79
Rhizanthella gardneri, 43
photo, 43
rhizome, 20
clip, definition, 128-129
definition, 128
Rhyncholaelia digbyana, 76
Rhynchostylis retusa, photo, 55
rock wool, 54, 55-56
root rot, repotting in cases of, 53
Ruiz, Don Hipólito, 19

salep, definition, 129
Sanderara, 91
scales, 60, 63
and humidity, 63
scape, definition, 129
Schomburgkia, photo, 137
seedlings, care of, 115
photos, 115
seeds, 18-19
distribution, 18-19
growing from, 113-115
starting, 113-115
selecting orchids, 35-40
for the greenhouse, 106
Selenipedium, 87
sepal, definition, 129
shade in the greenhouse, 105-106
sheath, definition, 129
slugs, 63
snails, 61, 63-65

Sobralia
photo, 18
leudoxantha, photo, 126
societies. *See* Orchids, societies
Sophrolaeliocattleya Jewel Box 'Black Magic' AM/AOS, 38; photo, 38
Sophronitis, 60, 70
coccinea 'Edelweiss,' photo, 2
specialization, 36
species, definition, 129
species orchids
importance of, 123
names, 34
species swarms, 19
definition, 129
sphagnum, New Zealand, 54, 55-56
spider mites, 60-63
and humidity, 61
spider orchid, 95. *See also Brassia*
spike, definition, 129
spraying to maintain humidity, 45, 61, 106
stamen, definition, 129
Stanhopea, 96
cultivation, 98-100
tigrina, 98
wardii, 98
stigma, definition, 129
structure of orchids, 17-18
Styrofoam, 30, 54, 55
summer care for outdoor orchids, 67
swan orchid, 96, 97. *See also Cycnoches*
sympodial
definition, 129
orchids, 20, 21

temperature
and light, 48-49
night, 49, 67
requirements, 23
requirements, cool-loving orchids, 60
requirements, and orchid selection, 35-37
requirements, phalaenopsis, 28
terrestrial, definition, 129
Thelymitra ixioides, photo, 119
thermometer, minimum/maximum, 45, 106-107
definition, 128
photo, 46
tobacco mosaic, 65
tortoiseshell orchid, photo, 91. *See also Oncidium ampliatum*
tree fern, 54, 55
trees, growing orchids on, 60
tribe, definition, 129
Trichopilia
suavis, 100
tortilis, 100
tuber, definition, 129

unifoliate, definition, 129

Vanda, 47, 67, 106, 112
cultivation, 98
photos, 21, 67
Bartle Frere x *V. Manila*, photo, 98
coerulea, 98
sanderiana var. *alba*, photo, 96-97
vanilla, 13
variety, definition, 129
velamen, definition, 129
vermiculite, 55
virgin orchid, photo, 76. *See* also *Diacrium bicornutum*
virus, 65-66
definition, 129
Vuylstekeara, 91
'Cambria Plush' FCC/AM/AOS, 91

Wardian case, 43-44
illus., 45
watering, 49, 57, 67
excessive, 51-53
phalaenopsis, 27
withholding, 48-49
wet season, 21
whiteflies, 63
wild orchids
habitat destruction, 117-123
importance of, 123
Wolfe, Nero, 15

Zygopetalum, 60